Essential
Gran
Canaria

by Gabrielle MacPhedran

Gabrielle MacPhedran, journalist and broad-caster, is the author of several guide books, including AA *Essential Berlin*, AA *Essential Canary Islands* and AA *Explorer Spain*. She is a regular contributor to the *Daily* and *Sunday Telegraph*, *The Times*, *Country Magazine* and other periodicals. She lives in Surrey with her travel-writer husband, Adam Hopkins.

AA Publishing

Above: *window in Mogán*

Page 1: *view over the rooftops of Fataga*

Page 5a: *the beach at Las Palmas*
5b: *local inhabitants of Barranco de Guayadeque*

Page15a: *colourful boats dot many fishing ports*
15b: *bust of Christopher Columbus*

Page 27a: *time-out at Puerto de la Aldea*
27b: *entrance to Mundo Aborigen*

Page 91a: *poster advertising the local pub in Artenara*
91b: *Sioux City*

Page 117a: *keeping a cool head at Barranco de Guayadeque*
117b: *exquisite example of Gran Canarian flora*

Find out more about AA Publishing and the wide range of services the AA provides by visiting our Web site at www.theaa.co.uk.

Written by Gabrielle MacPhedran

Edited, designed and produced by AA Publishing.
© Automobile Association Developments Ltd 2000
Maps © Automobile Association Developments Ltd 2000
Reprinted Nov 1998; Mar 1999
Revised second edition Jan 2000
Reprinted Aug 2000

Distributed in the United Kingdom by AA Publishing, Norfolk House, Priestley Road, Basingstoke, Hampshire, RG24 9NY.

A CIP catalogue record for this book is available from the British Library.

ISBN 0 7495 2368 9

Published by AA Publishing, a trading name of Automobile Association Developments Limited, whose registered office is Norfolk House, Priestley Road, Basingstoke, Hampshire, RG24 9NY. Registered number 1878835.

Colour separation: BTB Digital Imaging Ltd, Whitchurch, Hampshire
Printed and bound in Italy by Printers Trento srl

Contents

About this Book 4

About this Book

Essential *Gran Canaria* is divided into five sections to cover the most important aspects of your visit to Gran Canaria.

Viewing Gran Canaria pages 5–14
An introduction to Gran Canaria by the author
Gran Canaria's Features
Essence of Gran Canaria
The Shaping of Gran Canaria
Peace and Quiet
Gran Canaria's Famous

Top Ten pages 15–26
The author's choice of the Top Ten places to see in Gran Canaria, with practical information.

What to See pages 27–90
The five main areas of Gran Canaria, each with its own brief introduction and an alphabetical listing of the main attractions
Practical information
Snippets of 'Did You Know…' information
4 suggested walks
3 suggested tours
2 features

Where To… pages 91–116
Detailed listings of the best places to eat, stay, shop, take the children and be entertained.

Practical Matters pages 117–24
A highly visual section containing essential travel information.

Maps
All map references are to the individual maps found in the What to See section of this guide.
For example, Maspalomas has the reference ✚ 29D1 – indicating the page on which the map is located and the grid square in which the mountain is to be found. A list of the maps that have been used in this travel guide can be found in the index.

Prices
Where appropriate, an indication of the cost of an establishment is given by **£** signs:
£££ denotes higher prices, **££** denotes average prices, while **£** denotes lower charges.

Star Ratings
Most of the places described in this book have been given a separate rating:
✪✪✪ Do not miss
✪✪ Highly recommended
✪ Worth seeing

Viewing
Gran
Canaria

Gabrielle MacPhedran's Gran Canaria

Early Islanders
The word 'Guanche', literally 'man of Tenerife', does not, strictly speaking, apply to the aboriginal people of Gran Canaria, although it is widely used. The spirit of these early Canarios is everywhere and they have left their mark on the physical appearance, the names and sports of many present-day islanders. Even cave-dwelling has persisted, and pottery is still made exactly as it was in prehistoric days before the potter's wheel.

Fertile Fataga, an inland village surrounded by rocky hills

Most people come to Gran Canaria for its abundant sunshine and its golden beaches. They head for the south and the guaranteed rain-free resorts such as Playa del Inglés, Maspalomas and Puerto Rico. Here, the pleasures of sun and rest and recreation often prove so seductive that some never set foot outside their resort except to catch the plane back home. Thus they miss the one essential characteristic of Gran Canaria – its diversity.

Consider the geography: to the west, the island rises to cliffs of jagged black rock, pounded by a spume-laced sea. Among the northern hills, clouds can blot out the sun for hours at a time – an astonishment to southern habitués. Equally unexpected to some is the central range of volcanic peaks, the highest of which can attract snow in winter. From these rocky heights, forests of pine trees descend to hillsides spiky with euphorbia and prickly pear. The central valleys are lush and green, some of them extraordinarily fertile, with palms sprouting like feather dusters among mangoes, pineapple and papaya.

There is majestic landscape and rural tranquillity in abundance. But do not ignore the capital, Las Palmas, or the smaller towns. After decades of neglect by central government, greater local autonomy and European funds have recently resulted in a striking face-lift of the island and a growing self-confidence among its people.

Gran Canaria's Features

With an area of 1,532sq km, Gran Canaria is third largest of the seven major islands of the Canarian archipelago. The largest are Tenerife and Fuerteventura. Gran Canaria has the greatest population.

It is a circular, volcanic island which last erupted seriously about 3,000 years ago. The land comes steeply down from the high central peaks, with vast barrancos – dry water courses or ravines – running to the coast like the spokes of a bicycle wheel.

The capital city is Las Palmas, which is also capital of the province bearing the same name. This consists of Gran Canaria and the other eastern islands, Fuerteventura and Lanzarote. The western islands, including Tenerife, La Palma, Gomera and El Hierro, form the province of Tenerife. Together, since 1983, the two provinces have made up the Autonomous Region of the Canary Islands.

Position: in the Atlantic Ocean 210km from the African coastline, 1,250km from Cádiz.
Population: 650,000; 350,000 in Las Palmas.
Number of annual visitors: 2,200,000.
Highest point: Pozo de las Nieves (1,949m).
Wettest part: the north; average annual rainfall 500mm.
Average temperature: summer 24°C; winter 19°C.
Flora: the range of altitudes ensures the presence of plants from almost every climatic zone.
Fauna: the largest mammal is the rabbit.

Placing the Name
The name 'Gran Canaria' first appeared on a Spanish map in 1339. The historian Pliny the Elder (AD 23–79) called the island 'Canaria', a possible reference to the large dogs (from the Latin *canis*, 'dog') which he reported living on the island. It is unlikely that the native canary – a small brown finch with a poor singing voice – had anything to do with the matter.

Below: *Columbus House, Las Palmas*
Bottom: *volcanic stone and brilliant flowers*

Essence of Gran Canaria

Golden sands and blue seas are the essence of Gran Canaria for most visitors. But there are increasing numbers of people who come here to windsurf, sail, fish, ride, play golf, mountain-bike, fly aeroplanes, or paraglide. Walkers and botanists find the island irresistible. As for nightlife, there is enough choice of clubs, cabarets, pubs, discos and casinos to satisfy any taste, mainstream or alternative, and at any decibel level. But whichever way you choose to enjoy the island, those blue seas and golden sands are never far away.

The wide, man-made beach at Puerto Rico, ideal for family holidays

THE **10** ESSENTIALS

If you only have a short time to visit Gran Canaria, or would like to get a really complete picture of the island, here are the essentials:

• **Watch the sunset** over the sea from the lighthouse at Maspalomas (➤ 46–7). Anglers cast their lines from the rocks, shadows deepen among the dunes, children trail home across wide sands after a sundrenched day.

• **Take a boat trip** from Arguineguín (➤ 42) or Puerto Rico (➤ 60) to Mogán (➤ 48), last resort village on the west coast, for a view of the island from the sea.

• **Walk in the Tamadaba pine forest** (➤ 72) with soft pine needles underfoot and undergrowth of cistus and thyme. Look down to the harbour at Puerto de las Nieves (➤ 83), far below, and across the sea to Mount Teide on Tenerife.

• **Linger in the sun** at a terrace café in the Parque de Santa Catalina (➤ 38), in Las Palmas. Watch the locals play chess and dominoes at outdoor tables.

• **Make a weekend visit** to the Jardín Canario in Tafira (➤ 22). Bridal parties come in droves to be photographed in this verdant setting.

• **Visit the ancient religious site** of the island's aboriginal people at Cuatro Puertas (➤ 79). Look from the top of the windswept hill to imagine a time before the Spaniards arrived.

• **Have a coffee** in the lounge of the Hotel Santa Catalina (➤ 101) in Las Palmas. All celebrity visitors to the island stay here, including King Juan Carlos.

• **See a Canarian wrestling match**, or *lucha canaria*, a team sport descended from pre-Spanish, Guanche times which sends the restrained Canarios wild with excitement.

• **Drive eastwards from Pasito Blanco** (➤ 52) on the old coast road at night for a sudden view, as you crest the hill, of the lights of Maspalomas and Playa del Inglés, like a shimmering blanket of stars.

• **Catch a performance** of Canarian folk singing and dancing back in Las Palmas at the Pueblo Canario (➤ 112) on Thursday evening or Sunday morning.

Below: *beachside café at Maspalomas*
Bottom: *Tamadaba pine forest*

The Shaping of Gran Canaria

3000 BC–1500 AD
The island is inhabited by Cro-Magnon and Mediterranean-type stone age people, who wear skins, keep livestock and grow cereals. They have no written language.

1st century AD
First mention of the name 'Canaria', by the historian Pliny the Elder. He calls the archipelago 'The Fortunate Isles'.

13th century AD
Arrival of slaving expeditions from Europe.

1340–2
Portuguese and Spanish send expeditions from Mallorca.

1405
The Norman Jean de Béthencourt (see page 14) fails in his attempt to conquer Gran Canaria for the Spanish throne.

1478
Juan Rejón founds the town of Real de las Palmas and begins subduing the island. The aboriginal people are led by two kings: Tenesor Semidan, who rules the west of the island from

A tile painting of Columbus putting his fleet in to repair on the Canary Islands

his base at Gáldar, and Doramas, chief of the east, who rules from Telde. Rejón wins the first major battle.

1480
Under the Treaty of Alcáçovas, Portugal renounces her claims to the Canary Islands.

1481
The Guanche king Doramas is killed at Montana de Arucas.

1482
The Guanche king Tenesor Semidan is captured, taken to Spain and baptised as 'Fernando Guanarteme'. He then joins the Spanish cause.

1483
Siege of Ansite. Most Canarios surrender. Others throw themselves off cliffs. The end of aboriginal resistance.

1492
Christopher Columbus puts in at Las Palmas for repairs to his ships on his first expedition to the New World. He returns on his second and fourth voyages.

1496–c1525
Intensive colonisation by Spaniards, Portuguese and Italians. Portuguese bring knowledge of sugar cane industry from Madeira and Italians provide capital investment.

Early 16th century
Growing prosperity for Gran Canaria from trade with the New World and cultivation of sugar cane brought from Madeira.

The island becomes a target of British, Dutch and Portuguese pirate attacks.

18th and 19th centuries

After collapse of the sugar trade, following competition from the New World, main exports are wine and cochineal (the insects which produce the dye are bred and fed on prickly pear). Las Palmas becomes an important refuelling port for transatlantic shipping.

Early 19th century

Growing resentment at Spanish control, encouraged by ideas of American Independence, French Revolution and colonial liberation in Spanish South America.

1820

Las Palmas becomes the capital of Gran Canaria.

1852

The Canaries are declared a free trade zone in an effort to boost the islands' economy.

1882

Work begins on the harbour, Puerto de la Luz, at Las Palmas.

Early 20th century

Intensive cultivation of bananas and tomatoes is undertaken.

1927

Canary Islands are divided into two provinces, with Las Palmas de Gran Canaria as the head of the eastern province. Growing rural poverty results in illegal emigration to Latin America.

General Francisco Franco

1936

General Franco visits Gran Canaria and, from here, announces the launching of the military coup which begins the Spanish Civil War (1936–9).

1950s

Canarians demand home rule.

Bananas, still the principal crop in north Gran Canaria

1960s

Plans to develop the south for tourism.

1970s

Mass tourism arrives: tomato fields give way to hotels.

1975

Death of Franco.

1978

Spain becomes a constitutional monarchy under King Juan Carlos I.

1983

Spanish devolution leads to greater autonomy for the islands.

1989

Canary Islands become full members of the European Community (as part of Spain).

Peace & Quiet

Astonishingly, for an island as populous and popular as Gran Canaria, peace and quiet are easy to find. Even in the main tourist resorts, hotel gardens are often planted like miniature tropical forests.

Fishing off the harbour wall at Puerto de la Aldea, the westernmost part of the island

The West Coast

The major road through the southern resorts abruptly leaves the coast at Puerto de Mogán (► 24) and shoots up the barranco into the mountains. Any beach from Playa de Mogán to Puerto de la Aldea at the island's northwestern tip is likely to offer solitude.

The beaches of Veneguera (sand), Tasarte (pebble) and Asno (rock and black sand) are all accessible on foot. It is possible to walk to Güigüí, the star of all remote beaches, but only for the hardy and sure-footed. Make a deal with a fishing boat from Puerto de la Aldea, Mogán or Puerto Rico to drop you there and pick you up. In the summer, there are regular boat trips to Güigüí from Puerto Rico.

Inland Reservoirs

The reservoirs of Chira, Soria and Cueva de las Niñas, in the west central part of the island, offer areas to relax beside the water but away from the coast. In some places you can swim off a small beach or dive off rocks. It is possible to hike between all three reservoirs.

Walks

Several hiking groups offer accompanied walks in the more remote parts of the island. These are usually run by foreign residents and are often oversubscribed. If you walk alone, make sure someone knows where you are heading and can raise the alarm if necessary.

Native Plants

Gran Canaria is a botanist's delight, with a wide variety of vegetation. Common endemic species include the *Pinus canariensis*, or Canary pine, which has the useful talent of regeneration after fire: new growth emerges from seemingly lifeless, charred bark. The hard wood of this tree, called tea, is used for ceilings and balconies. The rock rose (*Cistus symphytifolius*) and asphodel (*Asphodelus microcarpus*) grow in pine forests.

The extraordinary-looking dragon tree (*Dracaena draco*), closely related to the yucca plant, has become the botanical symbol of the Canary Islands. With branches like the legs of a stumpy grey elephant, ending in a spiky green crown, this primitive form of plant life is extremely long-lived. Early Guanches dried the red resin of dragon trees, which they used as medicine and as a dye, and islanders still use it as a cure for toothache.

The Canarian palm (*Phoenix canariensis*), found all over the island, is similar to the North African date palm but shorter, with larger, lusher leaves and a more perfect crown. The leaves are used for basket work and the trunk for making beehives.

Below: *the orchid house at Palmitos Park*
Bottom: *a vital source of water – the reservoir at Soria*

Other endemic plants include the retama (broom), with yellow flowers in spring and summer; taginaste, which produces white or blue flowers in spring; verode, with pink or yellow flowers and tabaiba, a species of euphorbia, whose sap is used – with care – in popular medicine (it can cause temporary blindness). The cardón or candelabra cactus is a many-branched native euphorbia, technically *Euphorbia canariensis*. The sap is mixed with oil and used as a medicine.

Gran Canaria's Famous

Jean de Béthencourt

Charged by Henry III of Castile with the task of conquering the Canary Islands, this Norman soldier (1359–1426) set out in 1402 with his lieutenant Gadifer de la Salle and took the island of Lanzarote, for which he was awarded the title 'King of the Canary Islands'. He next conquered Fuerteventura. However, the aboriginal people of Gran Canaria resisted him successfully, and he returned to France, where he eventually died.

Christopher Columbus

Genoan-born Christopher Columbus (1451–1506) persuaded the Catholic Monarchs, Ferdinand and Isabella of Spain, to sponsor his expedition to find a western route to India. Instead of the Orient, he found the New World. On his first, second and fourth voyages across the Atlantic, Columbus put in at Gran Canaria. The house where he stayed and the church in which he prayed lie in the Vegueta district of Las Palmas (► 26).

Jean de Béthencourt, the failed would-be conqueror of Gran Canaria

Name-dropping
Other names the visitor may encounter which are famous on the island but not widely known elsewhere, include:
Nicolas Estévanez y Murphy, poet;
Francisco Guerra Navarro (Pancho Guerra), novelist;
León y Castillo, engineer;
Jose Luján Pérez, sculptor and religious painter;
Tomás Morales Castellano, poet;
Alonso Quesada, poet;
Josee Viera y Clavijo, historian and natural historian.

Benito Pérez Galdós

Pérez Galdós (1843–1920), the 'Charles Dickens of Spain', was the youngest child in a family of 10, born to an army officer and his wife in C/ Cano 6 in the Triana district of Las Palmas. The house is now a museum (► 31). He studied as a lawyer in Madrid before becoming a full-time novelist and playwright. The island is extremely proud of Pérez Galdós, although he lived his adult life on the Spanish mainland. His best known works include *Episodios Nacionales*, a historical novel in 46 volumes.

Néstor Martín Fernández de la Torre

Artist Néstor (1887–1938) studied at the Academy of Fine Art in Madrid but always kept his roots alive in the city of his birth, Las Palmas. Many of his canvases – such as *Poema del Atlántico* – depict aspects of the island in a romantic, free-flowing manner. See his work at the Museo Néstor (► 36) in the Pueblo Canario. He painted the murals in the Teatro Galdós, shocking bourgeois sensibilities and, less controversially, designed the Tejeda parador.

Top Ten

A COLON

COLON

LAS PALMAS DE GRAN CANARIA

15

1
Andén Verde

Andén Verde, or 'Green Platform', is the name given to a magnificent stretch of corniche road on the island's northwest coast.

Winding northeast along the cliff-face, the road offers thrilling glimpses downwards, by way of plummeting rock, to a vertiginously distant sea. Though the extent of the Andén Verde is a little vague, this most exciting part of the west coast effectively begins a short way north of San Nicolás de Tolentino (➤ 63).

Running just inland for 6km or so from San Nicolás, the road suddenly veers towards a gap in a hill-crest above the sea. There is a small car-park here, the Mirador del Balcón, or Balcony Lookout Point. Though views from the car-park are very fine, it is worth descending the few steps to a lower platform. From here, the rocks beneath, and the cliff foot to the southwest, may be seen clearly. The cliff is surmounted by a dramatic series of hills, each of them terminating suddenly in a triangle of dark cliff. Each successive triangle is a little lower than the one before, their diminishing height marking the descent towards the harbour at Puerto de la Aldea (➤ 56). The island of Tenerife lies west across the water.

The road continues to the northeast, following the cliff. There are one or two further spots where cars can pull off the road, sometimes with difficulty, so take care. As the Andén Verde draws to a close the road swings inland, descending towards the little village of El Risco.

View of the vertiginous coastline from the corniche road of the Andén Verde

2
Barranco de Guayadeque

An enchanting canyon southwest of the airport, on the eastern side of the island, and a centre of population in pre-Spanish times.

Lying between the municipalities of Ingenio and Agüimes, this barranco is more praised by environmentalists than any other on the island. From the flat floor of the dry river bed, the walls of the ravine rise through green terraces of cultivation, through tall palms, eucalyptus and the soft green ping-pong bats of prickly pear, to lofty crags of red volcanic rock.

Many of the island's rarest plants live here, and much of the barranco has been designated a nature reserve. The 80 endemic species of flora found here include the *kunkelliela canariensis* and *helianthemum tholiforme*.

The aboriginal people who once lived in this fertile valley left behind hundreds of caves, natural and man-made, that served as homes, animal shelter and grain stores. The many burial chambers found here form an important part of the Guanche exhibits of the Museo Canario in Las Palmas (▶ 33). The area is little inhabited today, but the 50 or so inhabitants are probably the most direct descendants of this prehistoric aboriginal world. They still farm, keep animals and live in caves. They even park their cars in cave garages. In Roque, the one small hamlet on the valley floor, there are cave homes, restaurants and a cave church. The area's most famous restaurant, however, is the Tagoror (▶ 94), right at the end of the barranco in a series of caves overlooking the valley. The stream beds under the trees make a pleasant and popular picnic spot during the weekends.

🕇 29E3

✉ Municipality of Agüimes: 30km south of Las Palmas, 28km northeast of Playa del Inglés

🍴 Several cafés in Barranco; Tagoror restaurant (££)

🚌 11 or 21 to Agüimes

♿ None

↔ Agüimes (▶ 42)

❓ Access on foot or by car from Agüimes or Ingenio (▶ 43)

Clearing the canyon's terraces for cultivation

3
Casa de Colón

✚ 35C1

✉ Calle de Colón 1

☎ 928 31 12 55

🕓 Mon–Fri 9–6, Sat–Sun 9–3. Closed public hols

🍴 Near by

🚌 30 from Maspalomas

↔ Catedral de Santa Ana (► 32)

A celebration of the great explorer: the interior of the Columbus House Museum

Once the governor's residence, this fine building now houses exhibits recalling the age of exploration.

When Juan Rejón founded the city of Las Palmas in 1478, among the first buildings he erected was a residence for the governor of the island. When Christopher Columbus arrived on the island on his first voyage of discovery in 1492, he presented his credentials to the governor and lodged in his house. This house, much restored and refurbished, is now the Casa Museo de Colón.

The house is built around two courtyards of elegant stone, decorated with Canarian balconies of dense, dark tea pine wood. Twelve rooms on two floors contain the permanent exhibition; those dealing with the four voyages of Columbus to the New World are the most fascinating. A copy of the log of the first journey is left open at the page referring to the stop for repairs in Las Palmas. Given the direction of trade winds and ocean currents, the island was and is a natural stopping-off point in any journey westwards. Subsequent generations have found it easier to travel between the Canaries and the Americas than to go in the other direction to mainland Spain. Cultural, social and familial ties have always been supplemented by ties of trade, and in times of economic trouble, many Canarios have found it more natural to emigrate to Latin America than to go to the mainland.

Among the intriguing displays are nautical maps, as fanciful and crude as a child's drawing; navigational instruments, ingenious and inventive but looking hopelessly inadequate to the modern eye; the tiny ships, and the names of the seamen who manned them. All recall the magnitude of the explorers' task and the courage needed to fulfil it.

4
Cenobio de Valerón

This network of around 300 caves is one of the most important archaeological sites of the pre-hispanic people of this island.

It was once thought that the complex, in a rocky cliff a few miles east of Santa María de Guía (➤ 85), was the abode of Guanche priestesses, or Harimaguadas, who served the god Alcorac; or that it housed young noblewomen in the period before marriage, when they were fed a calorie-rich diet in preparation for motherhood. Now, scholars agree that the caves were used as a fortified grain depository, indicating a high degree of social organisation.

The caves, under a red-yellow basalt arch like the upper jaws of a great fish, appear from a distance like a colony of swallows' nests, made up of round and rectangular chambers. They are reached by winding, steep stairs cut into the rock with the occasional platform.

Early writers described their astonishment on first seeing the Cenobio de Valerón, the round arch, the intricate complex of caves connected by steps and passages, and towers (now disappeared) at either side of the entrance overlooking the barranco. This was no mean achievement by people who had no knowledge of metal and used only stones and animal bones as tools.

Concerns for safety and the work of preservation have effectively put much of the complex out of bounds. It is no longer possible to clamber about inside the caves and explore the site. However, climbing up to this extraordinary place and seeing the evidence of the local 15th-century Stone Age culture is still a fascinating experience.

✚ 28C5

✉ Municipality of Santa María de Guía: 21km west of Las Palmas, 73km north of Playa del Inglés

☎ 928 38 13 68

🕐 Wed–Sun 10–5. Closed Mon & Tue

🍴 None

🚌 102, 103

✋ Free, but guard is pleased with a small gratuity

↔ Santa María de Guía (➤ 85)

The Cuevas de Valerón, a Stone Age granary tunnelled out of the cliff-face by the early indigenous islanders

5
Dunas de Maspalomas

✈ 29D1

✉ Maspalomas: 58km
south of Las Palmas,
6km south of Playa del
Inglés

🍴 Plenty of refreshment
places on and beside
the beach (£–£££)

🚌 Faro de Maspalomas is
a busy bus terminal.
Bus 30 is a frequent
direct service to Las
Palmas

♿ None

↔ Playa del Inglés
(► 54–5)

❓ Don't feed the fish in
the charco. Left to
themselves, they eat
the mosquito larvae and
keep this section of
coast mosquito-free

*The changing contours of
a sculpted landscape as
the sun sets over the
Maspalomas dunes*

*Spectacular sand dunes, part of a protected nature
reserve, lie right in the middle of the busy tourist
resort of Maspalomas.*

Together with the Charco de Maspalomas – a freshwater
lagoon behind the beach – and its associated palm grove,
the dunes form an area of natural beauty and ecological
importance to the south and west of Playa del Inglés and
Maspalomas. Their sands, composed of fine ground shells,
can reach a height of 10m and are spread over an area of
328 hectares, ending at the mouth of the Fataga gorge.

Far from being composed of moving ridges shaped by
wind, like the better known parts of the Sahara, these
dunes are made up of what seems to be a host of sweetly
contoured hillocks and surrounding valleys. It is a mildly
surreal but loveable landscape.

When plans were launched in the early 1960s, by the
Count of Vega Grande, local aristocrat and landowner, to
start building tourist complexes on this coast, special pleas
were made that the dunes should be protected from

development. The luxury Hotel Maspalomas Oasis and the Maspalomas Golf Course were early lapses from the path of environmental virtue. But there are hopeful signs that this extraordinary natural asset, right in the centre of the greatest tourist concentration on the island, now has enough champions to protect it from further depredation. Meanwhile, the dunes are advancing at the rate of a metre a year from left to right in the direction of the lighthouse.

In the *charco*, over 20 different species of birds have been observed in the past, and there are indications that the lagoon is being used increasingly as a stopping point during migration.

Making tracks across the dunes at Maspalomas, with mountains ever present in the background

6
Jardín Botánico Canario

29E5

Tafira Baja: 8km south
of Las Palmas, 53km
northeast of Playa del
Inglés

928 35 36 04

Daily 9–6

Jardín Canario
restaurant (££)

301, 302

None

Free

Caldera de Bandama
(► 78)

Occasional lectures

*Cactus in all its variety
is only one species of
endemic plant displayed
in the Jardín Botánico
Canario*

*This famous botancial garden in the Guiniguada
barranco reveals all that is spiky and smooth,
bizarre and beautiful of Gran Canarian flora.*

The garden was opened in 1952, with the aim of
preserving and displaying the many plant species endemic
to this island. Its first director was the Swedish botanist
Erik Sventenius, who did the preparatory groundwork of
finding and classifying, planning and planting – a task
assumed since 1974 by Dr David Bramwell.

The garden has two entrances, one at the top of the
150m-high barranco and the other at the flat bottom,
connected by paths and steps and taking you through the
different varieties of vegetation, planted at different levels.
Here is your chance to walk among Canarian palms and
the trees of the laurasilva forest that once covered this
island. The Jardín de las Islas displays all the most
important species of plants of the archipelago, and the
Cactus Garden has cacti from all over the world, with rare
examples from South and Central America. Endangered
species are carefully tended in two nurseries with the aim
of replanting them in their natural zones; there is also a
library for study and research.

At the top of the garden are the circular look-out point
and a white stone bust of historian and naturalist Don Jose
de Viera y Clavijo (the garden's official name is Jardín
Botánico Canario Viera y Clavijo). If you have managed to
get this far up from the bottom of the barranco, reward
yourself with some refreshment in the restaurant beside
the garden entrance.

7
Playa de las Canteras

This wide hoop of sand, over 3km long and protected by a natural rock barrier, is one of Las Palmas's most prized amenities.

Its position is extraordinary; backed by the hotels, shops and businesses of a major city, Las Canteras beach stretches in a golden curve, its comparatively shallow water warmed and sheltered from the wind by the presence of the inshore reef known as La Barra. A programme of improvements resulted in the planting of palm trees on the sands, and the re-building of a wide and attractive promenade, the Paseo de las Canteras, with attendant bars and restaurants, behind the beach.

Before mass air travel, visitors to Gran Canaria always arrived at Las Palmas by liner and tourism had its early beginnings in the north here, right behind Las Canteras beach. Older residents speak of a time when Las Canteras even boasted its own sand dunes, like Maspalomas, before the development of the town.

Summer weekends find the beach almost as crowded as those in the south of the island; its fans comprise foreign visitors and local Canarios who prefer the slightly cooler, occasionally cloudy days of the north, where the prevailing northeast trade winds form clouds as they hit the mountains. There is a good choice of hotel accommodation, pensions and apartments, many of them with sea views. As for restaurants and nightlife, visitors will find all they expect from a beach resort, combined with the usual offerings of a sophisticated modern city; but in the end, the beach itself is the star (▶ 39).

✚ 29E5

✉ Las Palmas

☎ Tourist Information Office at Parque de Santa Catalina, ☎ 928 26 46 23

🍴 Cafés on and behind the beach (£–£££)

🚌 1, 17, 23

⛴ Boats to Cádiz on Spanish mainland, jetfoil to Tenerife and ferries to all Canarian islands from passenger port

♿ None

↔ Vegueta (▶ 26)

The wide, sandy beach and the sheltered waters of Las Canteras, a step away from the city centre

8
Puerto de Mogán

28B2

✉ Municipality of Mogán: 81km southwest of Las Palmas, 29km northwest of Playa del Inglés

🍴 Many cafés in resort (£–£££)

🚌 01, 61

⛴ Lineas Salmon boat to Puerto Rico, Arguineguín

↔ Mogán (► 48)

Often referred to as Little Venice, Puerto de Mogán is a low-rise resort in the southwest of the island, complete with an attractive marina.

Until the 1980s this was simply a fishing village at the mouth of the Barranco de Mogán, providing shelter for a community of hippies and bohemians as well as for local residents. The hippies moved out – most unwillingly – as the first concrete mixers arrived to create a new tourist *urbanización*. Mutterings of rebellion against the continuing massification of the coast were silenced here, however, as apartments with prettily painted door and window surrounds, pedestrianised streets, canals and bridges and, above all, hibiscus hedges and roof gardens tumbling with bougainvillea, began to appear in the new Puerto de Mogán. Now, the resort is seen as an example of a tourist building style which does not violate the natural landscape.

Puerto de Mogán has a curved, grey, sandy beach protected by a breakwater, with sun beds and a beach restaurant, Tu Casa (► 95). The project was designed, however, for boating enthusiasts rather than beach lovers: the marina remains the main focus.

Throughout the day, passenger boats come and go between Mogán and other southern resorts. There are offers of fishing trips, sailing instruction and submarine jaunts. Chic shops and restaurants always seem full.

Come evening, the day trippers have gone and the town assumes a quiet, reflective air. Then, if a breeze stirs, you can hear the rigging rattling in the boats as you look up to the grandeur of the mountains behind (► 56–7).

Fishing harbour in the purpose-built resort of Puerto de Mogán

9
Teror

Surrounded by hills, this is a beautiful showpiece town, as well as the spiritual heart of the island.

White houses with exposed grey stone, dark wooden balconies, turned and decoratively carved, enchanting small patios hidden behind stern doors – this is the style of Canarian vernacular architecture which is revealed at its best in Teror. Elegant and well preserved, the town also has the distinction of accommodating, in its splendid main square, shaded with ficus and pine, the Basilica de Nuestra Señora del Pino – the cathedral of Our Lady of the Pine, the patron saint of Gran Canaria. On this site and in the branches of a pine tree, so legend goes, the Virgin appeared to the first bishop of Gran Canaria, Juan Frías, on 8 December 1492.

The interior of the church is grand, with stone columns, a wooden coffered ceiling, a gilt *retablo* or altar-piece shaped like the stern of a ship and above the altar, the 15th-century statue of the Virgin on a silver litter. The Virgin is traditionally dressed in the richest robes, regularly changed. She was also covered in a mass of precious jewels until 1975 when thieves made off with the treasure. They were never caught, and the incident is still a source of great anger and regret even to the most secular of Canarios.

Teror is an important place of pilgrimage to islanders all through the year but particularly during the fiesta of the saint on 8 September. Everybody converges on the town – on foot, donkey, car or cart – to offer prayers, fulfil religious promises, bring gifts of fruit and vegetables for the needy and – of course – to dance and sing the nights away. Every other week of the year, on Sunday mornings, a popular market is held behind the church (▶ 88).

Decorated wooden balcony at Teror

✚ 29D5

✉ Municipality of Teror: 21km southwest of Las Palmas, 77km north of Playa del Inglés

🍴 Several cafés in town (£–£££)

🚌 216

↔ Vega de San Mateo (▶ 90)

❓ 8 September is the feast day of the Virgen del Pino, celebrated throughout the island

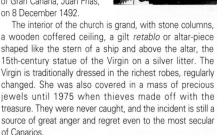

10
Vegueta

✝ 35C1

✉ Tourist Information
Office, Parque Santa
Catalina

☎ 928 26 46 23

🕐 Mon–Fri 9–2, Sat
9:30–12:30. Closed Sun

🍴 Many cafés in area
(£–£££)

🚌 30 direct from
Maspalomas

↔ Triana (➤ 34)

*Vegueta, the oldest part of Las Palmas,
contains a concentration of the most historic sites
of Gran Canaria.*

The cathedral of Santa Ana stands near the spot Juan
Rejón chose to found the Ciudad Real de las Palmas, the
Royal City of the Palms, on 24 June, 1478. A few palms
still flourish in the Plaza de Santa Ana, where children play
among the pigeons and pensioners sit chatting on the
benches. Two groups of bronze dogs, representing the
animals after which the island is named (according to one
theory) stand opposite the cathedral entrance.

The great explorer Christopher Columbus stayed in the
house behind the cathedral now called the Casa de Colón
(➤ 18). The church where he prayed before setting off on
his voyages of discovery, the Ermita de San Antonio Abad,
is also in the Vegueta, just behind the Casa de Colón.

The Vegueta is a place of surprising and delightful
smaller squares – among them the Plaza del Espiritu Santo
and Plaza de Santo Domingo. Stern mansions line the
streets, often decorated with traditional pine balconies –
for instance, C/de los Balcones, C/León y Joven, C/Herrería
and Mendizábal. The Montesdeoca restaurant, in the
street of the same name (➤ 92), is a revelation both archi-
tecturally and for its outstanding Canarian food.

Do not miss the excellent Museo Canario for a glimpse
of the life of early aboriginal people of Gran Canaria. For
modern life, a trip to the oldest of the city's markets, the
Mercado Municipal, is highly recommended.

*Pigeons strut in the palm-
lined square in front of
Santa Ana Cathedral, Las
Palmas old town*

What To See

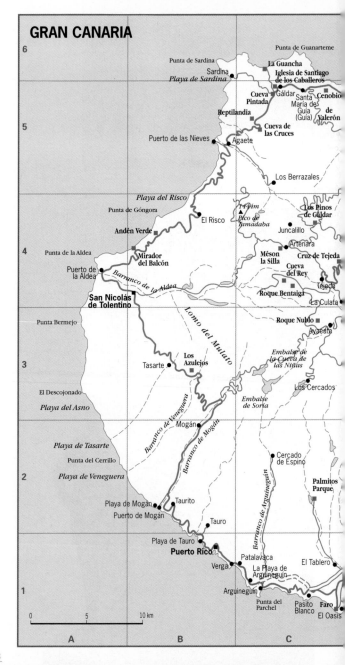

GRAN CANARIA

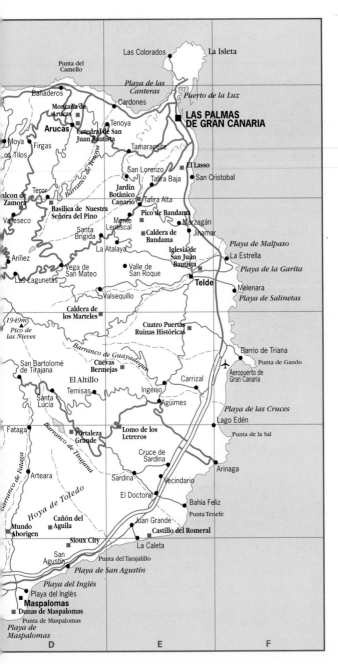

Las Palmas

Las Palmas, the largest city in the Canary Islands, lies like a long (14 km) and narrow ribbon on the island's northeast tip, barred from the sea by a highway. There are four distinct zones of interest: Vegueta, Triana, Ciudad Jardín and Playa de las Canteras. Vegueta, the monumental historic centre, adjoins Triana, a commercial district with fine examples of *modernista* architecture, a style of flowing curves and curious shapes. Ciudad Jardín (Garden City) is a leafy suburb created by British merchants in the 19th century, where you will find the Parque Doramas; and a quick hop across town takes you to Parque Santa Catalina and the splendid beach, Playa de las Canteras.

'Not without reason is the chief town of Gran Canaria called Las Palmas, for so many groups and groves of palms, with such superb stems, are to be seen nowhere else in the archipelago.'

HERMANN CHRIST
Spring Journey to the Canaries
(1886)

What to See in Las Palmas

CASA DE COLÓN ✪✪✪

Christopher Columbus stayed in this house while waiting for ship repairs during his first voyage of discovery to the New World in 1492. Originally 15th-century, but rebuilt in the 18th century, the house is now an excellent museum. Highlights include a life-sized reconstruction of the poop of the *Nina*, copies of Columbus's early charts and instruments, and a copy of the 1494 Treaty of Tordesillas, which effectively divided the undiscovered world between Spain and Portugal. There is also some excellent material on the history of Las Palmas. A small collection of 16th- to 19th-century paintings is on show, loaned from the Prado in Madrid.

🔲 35C1
✉ Calle de Colón 1
☎ 928 31 12 55
🕐 Mon–Fri 9–6, Sat–Sun 9–3. Closed public hols
🍴 Near by (£–£££)
🚌 30 from Maspalomas, 1 from Parque Santa Catalina
💶 Free
↔ Catedral de Santa Ana (▶ 32)

Left and above: *façade and detail, Casa de Colón*

CASA MUSEO PÉREZ GALDÓS ✪✪

The birthplace of the Canarian novelist, playwright and social critic, Benito Pérez Galdós, is now a museum and study centre. Born in 1843 in this fine town house built around a tiny patio, Pérez Galdós pursued a distinguished literary career on the Spanish mainland. Although he studied the influence of the old Guanche language on contemporary usage while he was a student, the island never featured in his writing – much to the disappointment of his compatriots. Exhibits on the first floor include the author's books, furniture made to his own design, a portrait of him by Sorolla and a re-creation of his study in Santander. When the museum first opened in 1964, a local bishop warned that a visit to the home of such a rabid anti-cleric might constitute a mortal sin.

🔲 35C2
✉ Calle Cano 6
☎ 928 36 69 76
🕐 Mon–Fri 9–1, 4–8, Sat–Sun 9–3
🚌 30 from Maspalomas, 1 from Parque Santa Catalina
💶 Free, conducted tour on the hour

- 35B5
- Calle Juan Rejón
- Tue–Fri 10–2, 5–9, Sat–Sun 10–2. Closed Mon
- Many cafés near by (£–£££)
- Playa de las Canteras (➤ 39)
- 15, 12, 13

- 35C1
- Plaza Santa Ana
- 30 from Las Palmas, 1 from Parque Santa Catalina
- Moderate
- Casa de Colón (➤ 18 and 31)

Diocesan Museum
- 928 31 36 00
- Mon–Sat 10–4:30. Closed Sun

Green on grey: the cathedral behind palms

CASTILLO DE LA LUZ ✪

This substantial fort, at the entrance to the Puerto de la Luz, was built in 1493 to defend the bay of Isleta against pirates. The English buccaneer, Francis Drake, was successfully repulsed in October 1595. Though the area is rather run down, there are continuing plans, to develop it and bring it back within the cultural life of the city. At the present time, it is used for temporary exhibitions.

CATEDRAL DE SANTA ANA ✪✪✪

A mixture of Gothic, Renaissance, baroque and neo-classical styles reflects the fact that, although this cathedral was begun in 1497, it has only recently been completed and cleared of scaffolding. The west front, designed by local architect, Luján Pérez, and completed in the early 19th century, faces the large, palm-lined square of Santa Ana and the two groups of bronze dogs which, some feel, gave the island its name (➤ 7). Because of building works, the cathedral is reached through the **Museo Diocesano de Arte Sacro** (Diocesan Museum of Sacred Art). Here there is a fine, if limited, collection of polychrome sculpture; otherwise the religious paintings and liturgical objects on display are generally unremarkable. The museum building and courtyard, however, are beautiful, and a real reward in themselves.

CENTRO ATLÁNTICO DE ARTE MODERNO (CAAM) ✪✪

This sparkling white gallery, housed in a grand mansion in one of the most picturesque streets of the city, opened in 1989 and shows the work of contemporary, mostly Spanish, some Canarian, artists. This is a surprisingly effective modern environment in an antique setting. Exhibitions are varied; the director is the noted sculptor, Martin Chirino.

✚ 35C1
✉ Calle de los Balcones 8–12
☎ 928 31 18 24
🕐 Tue–Sat 10–9, Sun 10–2. Closed Mon
🍴 Cafés and restaurants near by (£–£££)
🚌 30 from Maspalomas, 1 from Parque Santa Catalina
👐 Free

Did you know ?

It appears that the Guanches lost all knowledge of navigation and therefore did not travel between the islands. Boatless, they fished from the shore.

MUSEO CANARIO ✪✪✪

In this excellent museum, dedicated to the prehistory of Gran Canaria, we get a glimpse of the lives of the neolithic people who inhabited the island at the time of Spanish conquest. They were of proto-Berber, Cro-Magnon and Mediterranean stock, many of them tall and fair-haired. Exhibits show that they lived in caves, as well as stone houses. They kept livestock and grew cereal; they ground grain with millstones and used pestles and mortars. They mummified their dead – see the long gallery of skulls, skeletons and mummies wrapped in cloth of junco (cloth made of reeds) and goatskin. They were expert at leather and cane work and made fine pottery, without the benefit of the wheel. Although they had no written language, they left many examples of rock engravings depicting humans, animals and geometric symbols. The famous Painted Cave of Gáldar, closed to the public during conservation work, is reproduced in this museum.

The islanders were ruled by kings, or *guanartemes*, practised sports such as wrestling and cross-stick fighting (still popular among modern Canarios), and, according to contemporary accounts, they loved music and dancing. The first Europeans described the inhabitants as generous, simple and trusting. However, when it became clear that their visitors, armed with superior weapons (the Guanches had no knowledge of metal and had never seen a horse), were intent on invading and enslaving them, they resisted them with courage and skill. Indeed they kept up this resistance for most of the 15th century.

✚ 35C1
✉ Calle Dr Chil 25
☎ 928 31 56 00
🕐 Mon–Fri 10–8, Sat–Sun 10–2. Closed public hols
🍴 Good cafés near by (£–£££)
🚌 30 from Maspalomas, 1 from Parque Santa Catalina
👐 Moderate

Palm fronds for the faithful outside Santa Ana Cathedral

33

A Walk Around the Historic District

Distance
2.5km

Time
1½ hours strolling, four hours
with visits to attractions

Start point
Parque de San Telmo
⊞ 35C2

End point
Plaza de Cairasco
⊞ 35C1

Lunch
El Herreño (££)
✉ Calle Mendizábal 5
☎ 928 31 05 13

This walk starts at Calle Mayor de Triana, the shopping street that leads down to Vegueta, the old city. After visiting Vegueta, it returns to historic Plaza de Cairasco.

Walk south from the hermitage (ermita) of San Telmo on pedestrianised Calle Mayor de Triana.

Note the Art Nouveau buildings, starting at No 98.

Finally, angle left at the statue of Juan Negrín. At the major highway, go one block left to Teatro Pérez Galdós. Return and cross over to the market (Mercado de Las Palmas), on the left. Continue on along Calle Mendizábal, then right up handsome Calle de los Balcones.

Here, the local and national artistic heritage is on display at CAAM (Centro Atlántico de Arte Moderno, ➤ 33).

In Plaza del Pilar turn right, following the east side of the Colón house. At the next small square, the church of San Antonio Abad is to the right, and a few steps further down to the right is the Montesdeoca restaurant. Return and follow the north side of Colón house (entrance on left). Continue straight ahead into Plaza de Santa Ana and turn left, passing the cathedral façade.

The cathedral museum (➤ 32) is 25m left at the next turning, in Espiritu Santo.

Retrace your steps 25m to Calle Obispo Codina. Turn left and walk to Calle Dr Chil. Turn right.

The Museo Canario (➤ 33), is on the left.

Passing the Museo, continue briefly up Calle Dr Chil, then angle sharply back into Plaza de Santa Ana. From the cathedral front, exit left down Calle Obispo Codina. Cross the highway and go straight on into Plaza de Cairasco.

Here you can recover with a drink outside the Hotel Madrid, where Franco spent the night on the eve of the insurrection of the generals in July 1936.

LAS PALMAS DE GRAN CANARIA

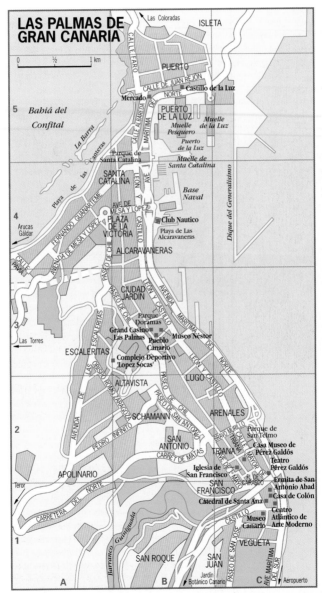

Las Coloradas

ISLETA

CALLE FARO

PUERTO

CALLE DE JUAN REJÓN

Castillo de la Luz

Mercado

NORTE

CALLE ALBAREDA

PUERTO DE LA LUZ

Muelle de la Luz

Muelle Pesquero

Puerto de la Luz

MARITIMA

5 *Bahiá del Confital*

La Barra

Parque de Santa Catalina

Muelle de Santa Catalina

Playa de las Canteras

SANTA CATALINA

AVE. LEÓN

AVE

CASTILLO

Base Naval

Dique del Generalísimo

AVE DE MESA Y LÓPEZ

4 Arucas Gáldar

FERNANDO GUANARTEME

AVENIDA DE MESA Y LÓPEZ

PLAZA DE LA VICTORIA

Club Náutico

Playa de Las Alcaravaneras

PASEO DE CHIL

ALCARAVANERAS

CALLE PAVIA

CIUDAD JARDÍN

LEÓN Y CASTILLO

AVENIDA

MARITIMA

DEL

3 Las Torres

DE LAS ESCALERITAS

Parque Doramas

Grand Casino Las Palmas

Pueblo Canario

Museo Néstor

NORTE

ESCALERITAS

PASEO DE CHIL

Complejo Deportivo 'López Socas'

LEÓN Y CASTILLO

ALTAVISTA

OBISPO PEDRO ZARAGOZA

LUGO

2

AVENIDA

DE

SCHAMANN

PASEO DE SAN ANTONIO

ARENALES

Parque de San Telmo

PEDRO INFINITO

SAN ANTONIO

CARRE. DE MATÍAS

BRAVO MURILLO

CALLE TRIANA

PL. DE

Casa Museo de Pérez Galdós

Teatro Pérez Galdós

APOLINARIO

Iglesia de San Francisco

TRIANA

CALLE MAYOR DE

PL. DE CAIRASCO

Ermita de San Antonio Abad

Casa de Colón

Teror

CARRETERA DEL NORTE

SAN FRANCISCO

Catédral de Santa Ana

Centro Atlántico de Arte Moderno

Barranco Guiniguada

CASTILLO

Museo Canario

1

PASEO DE SAN JOSÉ

VEGUETA

AVE. MARITIMA DEL SUR

SAN ROQUE

SAN JUAN

Jardín Botánico Canario

Aeropuerto

A   **B**   **C**

0   ½   1 km

35B3
Pueblo Canario
928 24 51 35
Tue–Fri 10–1, 4–8, Sun
11–2. Closed Mon, Sat
and public hols
Café in Pueblo Canario (£)
30
Modest
Pueblo Canario (➤ 39)

MUSEO NÉSTOR ✪✪

The life work of the island's most famous painter, Néstor Martín Fernández de la Torre, 1887–1938, is displayed in this museum in the Pueblo Canario. His best known work, *Atlantic Sea Poem* (two series of four canvases), is a celebration of the island's ocean environment. Néstor was pre-occupied by the effect of modern development on the island, reacting with angry denunciations and positive projects for retaining all that is best in Canarian architecture. There are examples of both in the museum. The Pueblo Canario itself is part of his resistance.

Sculpture of a Guanche pole-vaulter in Parque Doramas

35B3
Ciudad Jardín
Daily
Café in Pueblo Canario
and Hotel Santa Catalina
(£–£££)
30
Free

PARQUE DORAMAS ✪

This shady park, in the middle of Ciudad Jardín, contains the Hotel Santa Catalina, the Pueblo Canario and the Museo Néstor. Doramas, after whom the park was named, was the last Guanche king of Eastern Gran Canaria. In 1481, on Montaña de Arucas, he challenged the Spaniards to single combat and killed his rival with a javelin throw, but was fatally wounded himself. The Spanish and Guanche forces then joined in battle, but it was soon over. This was the final act of armed resistance against the Spaniards. Many of Doramas's followers hurled themselves off the cliffs, an event commemorated in the wild bronze sculpture in the hotel garden.

A Walk Around the Parks and Gardens

This pleasant walk around the delightful old city of Las Palmas takes you to the Pueblo Canario (Canarian Village) (► 39), Parque Doramas (► 36), the Ciudad Jardín (City Garden) and the modern shopping centre, before heading northwards to the lively Parque de Santa Catalina (► 38).

Start under the huge ficus tree to the southern side of the Pueblo Canario.

Within the Pueblo, the fine Museo Néstor (► 36) is to the right, the shops in front, and the outdoor café/restaurant to the left. Beyond the Pueblo is the Hotel Santa Catalina, which is worth a visit to admire its beautiful gardens.

Leave the hotel directly behind you, crossing the park (past the Doramas monument) to Calle León y Castillo. Turn left here, then second left up Avenida Alejandro Hidalgo. Take the first right into Calle Lord Byron, then wiggle through Ciudad Jardín to the far side. Take the first left up Jose Miranda Guerra, then the second right into Leopardi and continue, angling right along Calle de Brasil. Take the third left (Calle Rafael Almírez), one block, to turn right on to Pio XII.

The route is now linear until its last stages, with many variations of neighbourhood (and changes of road name). The first stretch is dull, but after about 10 minutes the route reaches a produce market, to the right, and then intersects with the major shopping street, Avenida Mesa y Lopez (Corte Inglés and Marks and Spencer are both to your right).

Cross over the street and continue straight along it as it quickly becomes Calle Tomás Miller.

Playa de las Canteras (► 39), the town's fine beach, lies straight ahead.

The walk then turns right two blocks before the beach, up pedestrian Ripoche to Parque de Santa Catalina.

Distance
1½ km

Time
1½ hours strolling; three hours with attractions and shopping

Start point
Southern entry to Pueblo Canario
🚩 35B3

End point
Parque de Santa Catalina
🚩 35B5

Lunch
Start with lunch at Bodegón in Pueblo Canario (£)

35B5
Santa Catalina
Many cafés around
(£–£££)
39
Tourist Information Office
☎ 928 26 46 23
Playa de las Canteras
(► 39)

PARQUE DE SANTA CATALINA ✪✪

The liveliest public space in Las Palmas, this park – which is really more of a city square – is surrounded by pavement cafés. Korean and Russian seamen mingle with African street-traders and tourists from northern Europe, while Canarians play chess and dominoes. Perfumeries and bazaar-like shops fill up the side-streets, which also act as a red light district by night. A four-storey Museum of Science and Technology is to be opened in the square. You will find the city's main tourist information office in a charming traditional Canarian building at the corner of the square.

35C2
Corner of Calle Bravo
Murillo and Avda Rafael
Cabrera
Many cafés around
(£–£££)
1, 11, 13, 9
Church open only during
services

PARQUE DE SAN TELMO ✪✪

A shady square full of tall palms and benches, this park is famous for its kiosk café, decorated in Modernista style with ceramic tiles from Manises, and for its charming small church, the Ermita de San Telmo (patron saint of fishermen). The church, decorated with a little Canarian balcony, was rebuilt in the 17th century after destruction by Dutch pirates. Inside, there is a fine *artesonado* ceiling and a baroque retablo. On the west side of the park, a stern neo-classical building guarded by soldiers is the headquarters of the Spanish army in the Canary Islands. It was from here that General Franco announced his opposition to the Republican government on 18 July 1936 and broadcast a rallying call to his troops, thus beginning the Spanish Civil War from which he emerged the victor in 1939. A bus terminus and taxi-stand make this park an important communications point.

> ### Did you know ?
>
> *An exclusive club, founded in 1844 (when its president was Englishman Robert Houghton), has its home in the neo-classical Gabinete Literario, in the Plaza Cairasco in Triana. With its playful modernista decoration, this is one of Gran Canaria's finest buildings.*

35B4
Alcaravaneras
Snack bars on beach (£)
71, 72

PLAYA DE LAS ALCARAVANERAS ✪

Las Palmas's second town beach after Las Canteras is a fine sweep of golden sand which has always suffered from its proximity to the port and the marina. Those suspecting the cleanliness of the water use the beach for sunbathing and beach football. Locals, self-styled 'fans of Las Alcaravaneras' would not go elsewhere.

PLAYA DE LAS CANTERAS   ✪✪✪

The 3km-long Playa de las Canteras, sheltered by the inshore reef of La Barra, is the city's premier beach, extremely crowded on summer weekends. The *paseo* behind the beach, with joggers morning and evening and walkers all day and much of the night, provides a fascinating indicator of a highly varied population. The major landmark of the area is the tall tower of the Sol Bardinos Hotel (➤ 23).

☩ 35A4
⊠ Santa Catalina
🍴 Cafés (£–£££)
🚌 1, 17, 23
ℹ️ Tourist Information Office
☎ 928 26 46 23
↔ Vegueta (➤ 26)
❓ Boats to Spain and North Africa, jetfoil to Tenerife, ferries to Canarian islands

PUEBLO CANARIO   ✪✪

The Pueblo Canario – the Canarian Village – is an attempt to preserve, re-create and display the best of Canarian architecture. A small group of buildings on the edge of Parque Doramas, based on the plans of the artist, Néstor Martín Fernández de la Torre (➤ 36), was erected after his death by his brother. There is a pretty courtyard, with outoor café tables, the restored Church of Santa Catalina, and a covered arcade of small shops selling Canarian handicraft – openwork tablecloths, musical instruments and Canarian knives with decorated handles.

☩ 35B3
⊠ Parque Doramas
🍴 Pueblo Canario Bodegón (££)
🚌 30
↔ Museo Néstor (➤ 36)
❓ Twice-weekly performances of traditional music and dance

TEATRO PÉREZ GALDÓS   ✪

Set on the edge of the busy carriageway that divides Triana from Vegueta, this theatre was designed by the architect Miguel Martín Fernández de la Torre and the murals (of Apollo and the Muses) painted by his brother Néstor in a style that shocked respectable theatregoers when they were first revealed. It is a haunt of the *haute bourgeoise* of Las Palmas.

☩ 35C2
⊠ Lentini 1
☎ 928 36 15 09
🍴 Cafés in area (£–£££)
🚌 1, 9, 11, 12

Teatro Pérez Galdós, on the edge of Triana

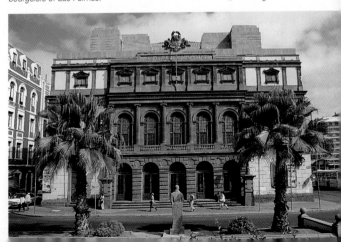

The South

In the south – which, for the purposes of this guide, extends from Gando airport in the east to Puerto de la Aldea in the west – the sun shines almost constantly. As a result the great resorts are clustered here, including San Agustín, Playa del Inglés, Maspalomas and Puerto Rico. At first sight they look like brash, concrete cities in a barren landscape. Then, little by little, their appeal becomes clearer: Playa del Inglés, divided from Maspalomas by spectacular sand-dunes; Puerto Rico, lively and friendly, Puerto de Mogán, calmer and beautifully planned; Playa de Taurito, dramatic and floral. All different, but all dedicated to pleasure.

The interior is barely 20 minutes' drive from any coastal point. Ridges of cindery, volcanic rock separate deep ravines. White villages provide oases of palms and olives, and, in springtime, a plenitude of almond blossom. Once discovered, this region is never forgotten.

' There are two islands,
ten thousand stadia from
Africa; they are called the
Isles of the Blessed. '

PLUTARCH
Life of Sertorius
(Ist–2nd century AD)

The South

✚ 29E3
✉ Municipality of Agüimes: 30km south of Las Palmas, 28km northeast of Playa del Inglés
🍴 Bar Casino Agüimes (£)
🚌 11 from Las Palmas
↔ Ingenio (▶ 43)
❓ Thursday market. Feast of San Sebastian 20 Jan; feast of the Rosary 7 Oct

Above: *a play on pastel in Agüimes*

AGÜIMES ✪

In the east of the island, at the mouth of the Barranco de Guayadeque, is the town of Agüimes, surrounded by terraced hills. This administrative centre of an area famous for fruit and vegetables was once, from 1483 to 1811, the seat of the bishops of Gran Canaria, whose citizens enjoyed privileges not extended to the rest of the island. The imposing neo-classical church of **San Sebastián** is testimony to its early importance. Unfortunately, the old heart of the town has largely been replaced by undistinguished modern buildings. A small square just above the church, surrounded by dark ficus trees, is a pleasant spot for civic events and festivities.

The area surrounding Agüimes, dotted with caves and cave dwellings, supported an extensive population in pre-Hispanic times. Today the town boasts a famous team of Canarian wrestlers, Unión Agüimes.

✚ 28C1
✉ Municipality of Mogán: 66km southeast of Las Palmas, 14km west of Playa del Inglés
🍴 Bar Cofradia de Pescadores, Avenida del Muelle, offers good fish meals (££)
🚌 01
↔ Puerto Rico (▶ 60)
❓ Tue market

ARGUINEGUÍN ✪✪

On an otherwise busy south coast, Arguineguín has for years been ignored by visitors – maybe due to the presence of a large cement factory on its outskirts. Now, hotels and apartments are being built for those who like the atmosphere of a lively little Canarian town. It has a good beach and, with an active fishing community, is famous for fish restaurants. Unfortunately, because the GC1 motorway ends here (at present), the town suffers from occasional traffic jams.

North of the town, the Barranco de Arguineguín, a fertile gorge planted with papayas, passion fruit and avocadoes, rises from a flat valley floor towards the heights of the central mountains at Ayacata (▶ 66).

ARINAGA ✪
A fast-growing, low-rise town with a lighthouse, a dark, rocky foreshore and a pretty Paseo Marítimo, Arinaga used to make its living from tomatoes and fishing. Now, many of its citizens are recent immigrants from inland villages who work in tourism-related industries. The coastline to the south is popular with dinghy sailors and windsurfers; the Bahía de Formas attracts migrating birds. A new harbour is being constucted but is not yet finished.

CASTILLO DEL ROMERAL ✪
This small, rather tatty, fishing village of low white houses is named after a castle which has long since disappeared. It is popular with those in search of simple but good fresh fish restaurants, many housed in former fishermen's terraced cottages.

INGENIO ✪✪
Ingenio is a large town and still growing. Its name means 'sugarmill' and recalls its early 16th-century history as a base for sugar production. The old town, spilling down narrow streets from the church of Our Lady of Candelaria, boasts some fine houses. Most visitors head straight for the northern suburb of Las Mejías and the **Museo de Piedras y Artesanía Canaria** (Museum of Rocks and Canarian Handicraft): it displays an indifferent collection of rocks but excellent handicraft, particularly the open threadwork or *calados*, and embroidery, *bordados*, for which this town and its neighbour, Carrizal, are famous.

> ### Did you know ?
> *Canarian wrestling* – lucha canaria – *is a competition between two teams of wrestlers dressed in T-shirts and shorts, and fought in a sand-covered ring. This is one of several sports in Gran Canaria with direct roots in Guanche tradition.*

Sidebar
- 29F2
- Municipality of Agüimes: 36km south of Las Palmas, 20km northeast of Playa del Inglés
- Cafés in town (£–££)
- 21, 22
- Barranco de Guayadeque (► 17)

- 29E2
- Municipality of San Bartolomé: 42km south of Las Palmas, 14km northeast of Playa del Inglés
- 05, 36, 61

- 29E3
- Municipality of Agüimes: 27km south of Las Palmas, 31km northeast of Playa del Inglés. Museo de Piedras y Artesanía Canaria: Camino Real de Gando 1, Ingenio
- Museum: 928 78 11 24
- Museum: Mon–Sat 8–6:30. Closed Sun
- Museum: small refreshment bar (£)
- 11 from Las Palmas
- Museum: free
- Fiesta of Virgen de la Candelaria 2 Feb

Ingenio, a centre for handicrafts

43

A Drive Around the Island

This long tour around Gran Canaria offers a glimpse of resorts, of the island capital, Las Palmas, and of magnificent volcanic scenery.

From Playa del Inglés take the coast road (not the motorway) to Arguineguín (11km).

The route leads through desert-like terrain. After Arguineguín (➤ 42), there follows a string of the newer resorts, Patalavaca (➤ 52) and Puerto Rico (➤ 60), a mass of matchbox constructions. Tauro and Taurito lead finally to Puerto de Mogán (➤ 56–7).

Fishing boats lined up at Puerto de Mogán

Keep right up the fertile barranco for Mogán itself (8km). Continue on the main road for San Nicolás (➤ 63) and Puerto de la Aldea (➤ 56).

Distance
Approximately 176km

Time
6 hours' driving, with possible detours

Start point
Playa del Inglés
➕ 29D1

End point
Playa del Inglés
➕ 29D1

Lunch
Los Remos (£)
✉ Avenida de los Poetas, Puerto de las Nieves

The Mirador del Balcón (Balcony Viewpoint, 11km from San Nicolás) yields magnificent cliff views, ushering in a thrilling corniche drive along the Andén Verde (➤ 16) to El Risco (10km).

Just before Agaete (16km), turn left (0.8km) to Puerto de las Nieves (➤ 83), with its fragile monolith beneath the cliffs: el Dedo de Dios, the Finger of God.

Inland from Agaete, there is a possible diversion up the pleasing Agaete barranco and down again (20–30 minutes). Gáldar (➤ 80) and Santa María de Guía (➤ 85) are unappealing from the road but repay exploration on foot.

Take the new highway from Gáldar to Las Palmas (➤ 30–9) or the old coastal highway through Guía. Enter Las Palmas by the tunnel; turn right at the sea front on the inner-city coastal highway (signs for Sur or South).

From here, the motorway follows the unappealing coast to Playa del Inglés (23km).

The little village of Juan Grande lies on the road between San Agustin and Vecindario

JUAN GRANDE ⭐

This small complex of church, manorial home and garden/palm-grove (open to pre-booked tours) belongs to the de Vega Grande family. The family's extensive estates consisted mostly of dry land, good only for growing tomatoes. But in the late 1950s it was Don Alejandro del Castillo, Count or Conde de la Vega Grande, who launched, in San Agustín, the first tourist development of southern Gran Canaria. By the 1970s the San Agustín/Playa del Inglés/Maspalomas resort was firmly on the tourist map and Gran Canaria had become a year-round holiday destination for northern Europeans. Tourism now accounts for 80 per cent of the gross national product of the island.

🛇 29E2
✉ Municipality of San Bartolomé de Tirajana: 40km south of Las Palmas, 12km northeast of Playa del Inglés
🍴 Fish restaurants in Castillo del Romeral (£)
🚌 01
↔ Castillo del Romeral (► 43)

LOMO DE LOS LETREROS ⭐⭐

The 'Ridge of the Inscriptions', in the Barranco de Balos, is a remarkable aboriginal site: a 300m-long rock face bearing incised sketches of the human form, and geometric patterns such as concentric circles, spirals and triangles. Much weathered over the years, it has also been considerably defaced. The etched shape of something resembling a boat is significant in view of the fact that, by the time they were conquered, the islanders had lost all knowledge of navigation and boating. The site is hard to find. Apply to the municipal offices at Vecindario (Calle Escorial 7, ☎ 928 72 72 00) for a map. Local environmentalists disapprove of open access. As with many of Gran Canaria's important archaeological sites, lack of funding and official neglect compound the problems created by graffiti-writers and souvenir-hunters.

🛇 29E2
✉ Municipality of Santa Lucía de Tirajana: 33km south of Las Palmas, 23km northeast of Playa del Inglés
🍴 Cafés in Cruce de Sardina (£–£££)
↔ Fortaleza Grande (► 68–9)
❓ Not open to public at time of writing

29D1

Municipality of San
Bartolomé de Tirajana:
30km southwest of Las
Palmas, 6km southwest
of Playa del Inglés

Cafés everywhere
(£–£££)

30 from Las Palmas

Playa del Inglés (➤ 54–5)

Aqua Sur

29D1

Ctra Monte León, km 3,
Maspalomas

928 14 19 05

Daily summer 10–6,
winter 10–5

On premises (£)

45, 70

Moderate

Below: *Lazy River at
Aqua Sur*
Bottom: *holiday
apartments surround a
pool in Maspalomas*

MASPALOMAS ✪✪✪

Although the twin resorts of Maspalomas and Playa del
Inglés have virtually merged into a single tourist conur-
bation, Maspalomas still has a more up-market image, no
doubt due to its magnificent dunes and the early building
of luxury hotels around the oasis.

The lighthouse (*faro*) and the bus and taxi terminus
mark the western boundary of the resort. From here a
promenade runs past small shops, bars and restaurants
and ends at the Barranco de Maspalomas, which, at this
seaward point, is occupied by a fenced-off lagoon (*charco*)
with reed beds, pampas grass and resident and migratory
birds. Environmentalists are making themselves heard in
the debate between developers and conservationists,
particularly in relation to the dunes and the lagoon, and
there is an Information and Interpretation Centre behind
the Hotel Riu Palace. Beach and dunes stretch eastwards
from here to join the sands at Playa del Inglés.

North of the lagoon, the barranco turns into a dry river
course with the prestigious 18-hole Maspalomas Campo
de Golf to one side. Estates of small, select apartments
soon give way to denser holiday accommodation, skirted
by wide avenues bearing the names of tour operators like
Tui, Thomson and Neckermann. The Faro 11 *centro
comercial* is a circular complex of shops, bars and restaurants. Amusement parks mark the resort's northern edge.

AQUA SUR ✪✪

This water park in the Barranco
Chamoriscan, north of Maspalomas,
offers 29 slides, a slow river, wave
pool, children's pools, a self-service
café and large car-park.

CAMELLO SAFARI DUNAS ✪

North of the *charco*, camel safaris are offered through the sand dunes. Riders sit on either side of their ungainly beast, managed by Paco and his friends, then trundle off in a circle that takes half an hour to complete. A safari package for large, pre-booked groups includes a cup of mint tea (sitting cross-legged in a fake bedouin tent) followed by the camel ride, then a bus trip up the barranco and lunch at a ranch.

➕ 29D1
✉ Avenida Dunas
☎ 928 77 20 58
🕐 Daily 9–5
🍴 Nearest café on beach (£)
🚌 Plaza del Faro, 29, 30, 32
💷 Moderate

HOLIDAY WORLD ✪✪

This funfair is a Maspalomas landmark by night, blazing with lights. The entrance fee covers all rides, which include a ferris wheel, boat-shaped swings, giant see-saws, pirate ships, dodgem cars, bouncing castles, tombola, snooker and parrot and sea-lion shows. Fifteen minutes in the laserdrome, a fantasy battleground with loud, atmospheric music, costs extra and requires a minimum of 11 and a maximum of 32 players.

➕ 29D1
✉ Campo Internacional
☎ 928 76 07 99
🕐 Daily from 5PM in summer, 6PM in winter
🍴 Cafés on premises (£)
🚌 Salcai 29, 30, 32, 36, 45, 70
💷 Moderate
❓ Car park

KARTING MASPALOMAS ✪

Karting Maspalomas is a Go-Kart track, marked by banks of blue-and-white tyres, almost opposite Aqua Sur water park. Payment is by every 10 laps. Spectators sit behind the large windows of the bar assailed by loud rock music inside and the squeal of tyres outside.

➕ 29D1
✉ Carretera Monte León
☎ 928 14 12 38
🕐 10AM–11PM
🍴 Café-bar (£)
🚌 45, 70 💷 Expensive

OCEAN PARK ✪

This water park has no fewer than 13 slides, six of them designed specifically for children, as well as a wave pool, lake and games rooms – all in all, plenty of action to occupy any children or adults who have exhausted the attractions of the beach.

➕ 29D1
✉ Campo Internacional
☎ 928 76 43 61
🕐 Daily 10–5
🍴 On premises (£)
💷 Moderate

47

MOGÁN

✚ 28B2
✉ Municipality of Mogán: 88km southwest of Las Palmas, 37km northwest of Playa del Inglés
🍴 Cafés in town (£–£££)
🚌 38
↔ Puerto de Mogán (► 56–7)
❓ Town fiesta first Sunday in August (Feast of San Antonio el Grande)

Mogán lies some 10km inland from the sea and its own harbour, Puerto de Mogán. The barranco running between the two is rich with tropical fruits; the slowly climbing road is lined almost continuously with hamlets. Numerous houses here are built in traditional rustic style, with large stones emerging through white rendering to create an attractive piebald effect. The little white town itself is comfortable and of some importance: it is from here that the whole district, including the coastline from Arguineguin to Puerto Mogán and even further west, is governed.

MUNDO ABORIGEN

✚ 29D2
✉ Carretera de Fataga
☎ 928 17 22 95
🕐 Daily 9–6
🍴 Café and souvenir shop on premises (££)
🚌 18
👋 Moderate
↔ Arteara (► 66)

This open-air museum recreates a stone-age settlement spread across the upper hillsides of the Barranco de Fataga. Life-sized figures of early Guanches occupy caves and stone-built houses, milling flour, cooking, performing a trepanning operation or participating in a religious ceremony. Their social hierarchy, their system of agriculture and knowledge of medicine – herbs, surgery, mummification – are clearly demonstrated and explained in Spanish, English and German.

Mundo Aborigen is based on the chronicles of the first invaders, who found the aboriginal people living in well-organised, close-knit communities. They are invariably described as gentle and kindly, lovers of sport and music and redoubtable in battle.

The spirit of the Guanches is most strongly evoked in the beauty of the hillside and the views from this spot. To the west, dark striated gorges recede into the distance, and to the south, at the mouth of the barranco, lies the white city of Playa del Inglés and the Maspalomas dunes.

Model of an early island inhabitant in the Mundo Aborigen open-air museum

Did you know ?

The early aborigines were great pole-vaulters – a useful skill in ravine country. Modern Canarios still use poles called lanzas or garottes, 3m long and ending in a steel point. Shepherds use them at work, but most are used in sport.

PALMITOS PARK

★★★

Spread over 200,000sq m at the head of the Barranco de Chamoriscán, this park is one of the island's principal attractions. Exotic birds – 230 different species, many of them uncaged – include flamingoes, toucans, cranes, macaws, hornbills, peacocks and tiny hummingbirds.

Winding paths lead from one point of interest to another past a stream, a palm grove (there are 51 varieties among 1,000 palms), clumps of giant euphorbia, to a small island, home to a couple of white gibbons. The heated butterfly-house has butterflies from all over the world, and the orchid house, said to be the first in Spain, is also spectacular. There are plenty of shady benches and cafés.

The park opened in the 1970s and has been regularly extended and improved. Recently a new 1,000sq m aquarium was added in a dramatic natural setting, with vast concave glass tanks set in rock surrounds, providing a panoramic view. Tropical fish from the Pacific region and the Amazon are on view here.

A favourite with children is the parrot show, included in the price of entry. A well-trained troupe of macaws walks tightropes and rides bicycles to enthusiastic applause.

✚ 28C2

✉ Barranco de Chamoriscán: 55km southwest of Las Palmas, 15km northwest of Playa del Inglés

☎ 928 14 02 76

🕐 Daily 9–6

🍴 Cafés and souvenir shops in park (££)

🚌 Free bus services from Playa del Inglés, San Agustín and Puerto Rico

💰 Expensive

↔ Aqua Sur (➤ 46)

❓ Parrot shows on the hour 11–5, last show 5:45

There is far more to see than palms in Palmitos Park, as this barranco *garden reveals*

In the Know

If you only have a short time to visit Gran Canaria, or would like to get a real flavour of the island, here are some ideas:

10
Ways To Be A Local

Smile – Canarios give an initial impression of shyness and reserve which disappears with the first smile.

Eat late. Lunch may not start until 2 and dinner not until 8, particularly away from the tourist resorts.

A Canario surveys the world with equanimity

Don't just rely on the menu in a Canarian restaurant. For best results, ask them what they are cooking.

Reserve beachwear for the beach if you do not want to look out of place.

Be ready to pick up hitchhikers in the country. Some roads are relatively new and drivers have always offered lifts.

Take warm clothing if you are out for the day. Temperatures change fast.

Let your children be spoiled. Canarios love children.

Try speaking Spanish, however badly. It goes down well.

If the weather looks overcast, drive to another part of the island.

Don't get drunk: it's considered very bad form.

10
Good Places To Have Lunch

Casa Montesdeoca, Las Palmas (£££) Montesdeoca 10 ☎ 928 33 34 66. Patio and ground floor of a restored mansion in the old town. Wonderful ambience, great food.

Casa Romántica, Agaete (££) ✉ Valle de Agaete, km 3.5 ☎ 928 89 80 84. Excellent international and Canarian food. Ice cream with fruit from the garden.

Chipi-Chipi, Playa del Inglés (££) ✉ Avenida Tirajana, Ed. Barbados 1 ☎ 928 76 50 88. Good food, well served, in an unpretentious restaurant.

Cho Zacarías, Vega de San Mateo (££) ✉ Avenida Tinamar ☎ 928 66 06 27. Canarian dishes in a museum of Canarian rural life.

Cofradía de Pescadores, Arguineguín (££) ✉ Avenida del Muelle ☎ 928 15 09 63. A fishermen's co-operative with an island-wide reputation. Freshest of fish and seafood.

A camel safari makes its way through a barranco

El Herreño, Las Palmas
(££) ✉ Mendizabal 5-7
☎ 928 31 05 13. Busy bar
and ample dining rooms
serve good food and wine
from the island of El Hierro.

Gran Buffet Las Camelias
(£) ✉ Playa des Inglés,
Avenida Tirajana 15 ☎
928 76 02 36. A self-service
restaurant with a good
variety at reasonable prices.

Hipócrates, Las Palmas
(££) ✉ Calle Colón 4,
Vegneta ☎ 928 54 82 51.
Vegetarian restaurant in the
old town. Good service,
pleasant atmosphere.

Shikhara, Playa del Inglés
(££) ✉ Avenida Tirajana
17, Ed. Barbados II ☎ 928
76 33 68. Indian restaurant
popular with vegetarians as
well as carnivores.

Viuda de Viera, Ayacata
(£) ✉ Cruce de Ayacata
☎ 928 12 73 94. A
roadside restaurant
overlooking a valley. Well-
cooked, simple food.

🔟 Top Activities

- Camel riding
- Deep-sea fishing
- Diving
- Go-Kart racing
- Golf
- Horse-riding
- Paragliding
- Sailing
- Walking
- Windsurfing

For addresses and
telephone numbers
(► 114–15)

🔟 Top Souvenir Ideas

- Basketwork
- Black felt Canarian hat
  (*cachorro canario*)
- Canarian cigars
- Decorated Canarian
  knife
- Embroidery work
- Pottery, unglazed, hand-
  made
- Rum from Arucas
- Seeds of Canarian plants
  (in packets)
- Shepherd's woollen
  blanket
- Traditional stringed
  instrument (*timple*)

🔟 Top Views

- Ayacata in almond
  blossom (February)
- Bandama Golf Course,
  seen across the crater
- Fortaleza rock (ancient
  Ansite), from main road
  south of Santa Lucía
- Maspalomas dunes,
  from sky-diving
  parachute
- Moya, from the west
  side of the barranco
- Puerto de Mogán, from
  the sea
- Roque Bentaiga, from
  Artenara
- Roque Nublo, from most
  points in the island
  centre
- Tenerife, from
  Tamadaba pine forest
- Wild west coast, from
  Mirador del Balcón

*Novice windsurfers take
to the water*

28C1

Municipality of San
Bartolomé: 57km
southwest of Las Palmas,
5km west of Playa del
Inglés

Restaurant in camping
site behind marina at
Pasito Blanco (£)

32, 61

Arguineguín (➤ 42)

*A line-up of boats in the
marina at the small
southern resort of
Pasito Blanco*

PASITO BLANCO

This attractive complex of houses, yacht club and marina
lies in a sheltered bay just west of Maspalomas. Though it
is private, the public may walk down from the 812 highway
into the resort to swim off the small beach to the right of
the jetty, or dive off the rocks into Pasito Blanco's
famously clear waters. Fifteen minutes' walk along the
track to the west brings you to Playa de las Mujeres,
where nude bathing is common and people occasionally
camp out (illegally) at night. From here, another 30-minute
walk brings you to the Playa de la Arena, but there are no
shops or beach bars on the way.

A track in the opposite direction from Pasito Blanco,
towards Maspalomas, brings you first to a fine sandy
beach, Playa del Hornillo, and then to Las Meloneras, a
wide, curved beach with a growing tourist development.
The luxury Riu Palace Meloneras Hotel has already opened
its doors and the building of a new marina, golf course,
conference centre and Canarian village is planned. The
shining globe in the arid hills above Pasito Blanco, visible
from the road, is the NASA space tracking station, the
Estación de Seguimiento Espacial de Maspalomas.

28C1

Municipality of San
Bartolomé de Tirajana:
68km southwest of Las
Palmas, 16km west of
Playa del Inglés

32, 61

Arguineguín (➤ 42)

52

PATALAVACA

Patalavaca, literally 'Cow's Foot', is reputed to have the
longest hours of sunshine on the island; it also offers a
beach of light-coloured sand and flat rocks. Not surprisingly, this small resort is dense with steeply rising hotels
and apartment blocks. The clientele is mostly
Scandinavian. A new coastal walkway now connects
Patalavaca with its neighbour, Arguineguín.

A Walk Around Playa del Inglés

This walk follows the coastal promenade from San Agustín (➤ 62) to Playa del Inglés (➤ 54), and continues along the beach, around the Maspalomas dunes, to end at Maspalomas lighthouse. There is no shade on the beach; walk early morning or late evening.

Start from the grey–sand beach at San Agustín, taking the recently improved promenade to the right, past hotel gardens at first, then apartments.

Climbing a little above rocks, the path circles round to the beach of Las Burras, where a few fishing boats rest on the sands. The hotels of Playa del Inglés are now firmly in view.

Approaching along the promenade, pass a series of fishermen's shacks to the left.

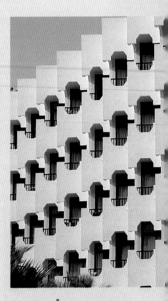

One shack is the Bar Pérez, serving bocadillos (bread rolls with filling), salad and beer.

Passing the Europalace Hotel, the promenade ascends several flights of steps to follow the top of a modest cliff. At the centre of Playa del Inglés, it descends again to cross the only road along the route (Avenida de Alfereces Provisionales). Turn left along the road on to the beach, by now golden in colour, then follow the beach to the right.

Narrow at first, it soon expands into a wide wedge, with beach beds and beach bars and, towards the end, a nudist zone. Behind, the golden dunes now rise, not in long ridges but in individual hillocks.

Follow the fringe of beach around the dunes. Twenty minutes from the corner brings you to Maspalomas. Pass the freshwater pond to the right, then keep to the sea for the lighthouse.

San Agustín remains an attractive resort despite tourism

Distance
8km

Time
2½ hours

Start point
San Agustín
🚼 29D1

End point
Maspalomas
🚼 29D1

Lunch
El Señador beach bar (£), before the lighthouse

29D1
Municipality of San
Bartolomé de Tirajana:
52km south of Las
Palmas. Tourist
Information Office:
Centro Comercial Yumbo
Tourist Office: 928 76 25
91
52 from Las Palmas
Maspalomas (► 46–7)

PLAYA DEL INGLÉS

The first sight of Playa del Inglés, as you swing south on the motorway from the airport, is not reassuring. It has all the marks of haphazard, unplanned and hastily assembled hotels and apartments in a concrete sprawl.

Once inside the resort, the first-time visitor is likely to get lost among identical streets with identical hotels. There is no obvious town centre, no charming plaza with shady trees and outdoor cafés, of the kind that you will find in any true Canarian town. Most of the life, apart from that of beach and hotel, is concentrated in the rather grim commercial centres (*centros comerciales*). These are buildings of several storeys, often with one or two below ground level, containing hundreds of small units of shops, bars, restaurants and entertainments. They are worth visiting only in the evening, when they become animated; and even then, they may become too animated for some tastes.

On the plus side of Playa del Inglés, the sunshine is almost guaranteed, the beach is splendid and the resort has plenty of everything most tourists want: accommodation in every category, from *grand luxe* to cheap *pension*, restaurants to suit every palate and purse and representing every national cuisine, with diversions – again, to suit all tastes – for every hour of the day and night.

It is also well-served with buses, a legion of taxis and car hire agencies and even a miniature train, so that moving around, or out of, Playa del Inglés, is a simple matter. Recently, a great deal of money has been spent on planting trees and flowers in public areas.

The cave-shaped Ecumenical Church of San Salvador, in Playa del Inglés

The nearest thing to a town centre in Playa del Inglés is the vast, rectangular complex of the Yumbo Centrum with the main Tourist Information Office at its southeastern corner on Avenida de Estados Unidos. The Yumbo, the largest of 11 such centres in Playa del Inglés alone (among them the Cita, Sandía, El Veril, Gran Chaparral), is a vast bazaar of cheap clothes, leather, souvenirs, electronic goods and perfumes. Of the many bars, restaurants and entertainments on offer on its four floors, a substantial number now caters for the gay community. The focus of young nightlife (which begins after 10PM) revolves around the *centros comerciales* like the Kasbah or the Metro grouped around the Ecumenical Church of San Salvador, on Calle de Malaga.

In the early evening, the heart of Playa del Inglés is the long coastal promenade, the Paseo Costa Canario, which runs the length of the coast from San Agustín (► 62) to Maspalomas (► 46–7).

The district of San Fernando lies north of Playa del Inglés, bounded by the 812 highway and the GC1 motorway. This area is home to Canarian workers in the tourist industry. For the visitor, it provides the best chance of eating in local *tapas* bars and restaurants at local prices and – for self-caterers – of stocking up on groceries at prices lower than in the resorts. There is also a Canarian wrestling stadium beside the football ground.

Did you know ?

Most winter visitors to Playa del Inglés are German, some are Scandinavian. The British, and mainland Spaniards, tend to holiday here in the summer.

Modern Playa del Inglés, formerly tomato fields

Above: *Puerto de la Aldea, a picture of tranquillity – until the September fiestas*

PUERTO DE LA ALDEA ✪✪

The little harbour town of Puerto de la Aldea, sheltering under a mountainous cape to the north, was long the only practical means of reaching San Nicolás de Tolentino (➤ 63), just inland. The *puerto* has a small selection of fish restaurants and a promenade, with distant views of Tenerife, leading south along the rocky beach. Behind, among pine trees, is an extensive *merendero* (picnic area), with tables and seating. Beyond, in the barranco bed, lies a fresh-water pond, or *charco* – the finishing point of the famous *bajada de las ramas* ('bringing down of the branches'), celebrated each September. In a ceremony of pre-Hispanic origin, local people would bring down palm branches and beat the water with them in the hope of rain, or possibly as a fertility rite. In 1766 the local bishop was excommunicated for tolerating the *bajada*. Nowadays, it is more of a water festival, with much excited leaping and splashing in the *charco*, brandishing bunches of vegetation and dancing to the band.

PUERTO DE MOGÁN ✪✪✪

This small but attractive town marks the present westerly limit of tourist development on the island. Thoroughly modern though it is, many day trippers come, often by boat with the Lineas Salmón company, to enjoy its old-fashioned, Mediterranean atmosphere. Puerto de Mogán offers the gentle pleasures of strolling through floral lanes, window-shopping, watching the bustle in the marina and fishing harbour and eating at waterside restaurants.

If you continue strolling to the very end of the harbour, the views out to sea from the (not very high) terrace of the El Faro (The Lighthouse) bar/restaurant make it a pleasure to linger over a drink.

Diversions include a trip in the Yellow Submarine, a genuine submersible (free bus service from major resorts). You can gaze at the splendours of the deep for 40 minutes out of your very own porthole. For the more active, the choice extends from diving (day or night), or learning to dive, to sailing (mono-hull or catamaran, with or without a skipper) and deep sea sport fishing for marlin, tuna or barracuda. Shark fishing is also popular here. Trips usually last for about six hours and the price includes bait, tackle, rod and reel. Spectating passengers pay a reduced price.

Puerto de Mogán – the most westerly resort in Gran Canaria and, some say, the loveliest

Puerto de Mogán also has an excellent sandy beach. If you want some exercise followed by a quiet swim, you could walk along the road (looks closed, but is not) from the village to the next beach westwards at Veneguera. There are plans to build an *urbanización* there.

Did you know ?

Schools of whales and dolphins are a common sight in these waters. The best way to spot them is on summer boat trips.

To the east from Puerto Mogán to Puerto Rico, there is a series of beaches: Playa de Taurito, sandy with swimming pools, landscaped gardens and a smart *urbanización* or residential area; Playa del Cura, a growing *urbanización*, with much fresh construction underway, and a dark, sandy beach; and Playa de Tauro, a sandy beach, with the Guantanamo camping site straddling the road and a number of small houses to let (► 24).

Food & Drink

Spaniards love eating out, and Canarians are no exception. Given the number of visitors here, it is no surprise that the island offers every kind of Spanish and European food. But Canarian food is rather different: country cooking, revealing a deep love for the island's own ingredients.

Main Dishes

Top of the list and found everywhere are *papas arrugadas* ('wrinkly potatoes'). These are small potatoes, boiled in their skins in water and coarse salt: 'saltier than the sea', says one local recipe book. They are eaten with a sauce called *mojo*. *Mojo verde*, or green *mojo*, is made with oil and vinegar, garlic, cumin, coriander and parsley; in *mojo rojo*, or red *mojo*, paprika is substituted for the coriander and parsley; and there is *mojo picon*, with a bracing dose of chilli. Taste before you dollop, especially the red varieties. These sauces are also served with fish and meat.

Less obvious to the visitor, since it is not often served in restaurants, is a form of cereal called *gofio*. Essentially this is any cereal – typically wheat or maize – toasted, then milled, and served either as a breakfast-type cereal with milk; moistened and made into little balls (a dumpling substitute); as a thickening in stews and soups, or as an addition to almost any kind of drink. This is the essential food of home and hearth. Most Canarians are addicted.

Other rustic dishes on the Gran Canarian menu include rabbit, usually served in stews, and hearty *sancocho*, a great favourite in bars and simple eateries. *Sancocho* consists of salt fish, usually in chunks, soaked and boiled, and served with *papas arrugadas*, *mojo* sauce and balls of *gofio*.

As may be expected, fresh fish is served in many places, especially in fishing villages. This, with or without

Paella, Spain's most famous dish, is always good value

58

mojo, is something that should not be missed. Cheese is also produced in a number of villages, most notably *queso de flor* ('flower cheese'), a light goat cheese scented with artichoke flowers.

Asparagus and avocadoes are grown in many areas of the island.

Island Drinks

On an island where fruit is mostly tropical and sub-tropical – mangoes and papaya are common – the local fruit juice is well worth tasting; and Gran Canaria also boasts its own excellent mineral waters.

Of other drinks, wine is produced in small quantities, especially in the Bandamas area, around Santa Brígida. A number of *bodegas* are to be found in and around Monte de Lentiscal, and quality is said to be improving. In San Bartolomé de Tirajana a local liquor called *guindilla* is made from the sour cherry or *guinda*. A lemon-flavoured liquor called *mejunje* is made in Santa Lucia. More popular across the island is local rum, *Arehucas*, made in Arucas on a base of sugar cane. Canarian workers are very inclined to take a shot of it at breakfast time.

Above: fresh seafood is always on the menu
Below: pork is usually served as a casserole or stew

Canarian Desserts

On Gran Canaria desserts are not a culinary adventure. Apart from *flan*, a custard pudding popular throughout Spain, the local speciality is *bienmesabe* ('how good it tastes'). Made from almonds and honey, it is often used as a sauce poured over ice cream. Nougat and marzipan are other local products.

🔲 28B1

✉ Municipality of Mogán:
72km southwest of Las
Palmas, 20km west of
Playa del Inglés

🍴 Choice of beach and
town restaurants (£–£££)

🚌 31, 39

🔄 Mogán (➤ 48)

PUERTO RICO ✪

They say there will be no new building in this brash and
thrumming resort because there is no room left – not for
the tiniest hotel, nor the smallest apartment.

Puerto Rico grew up on the strength of its constant
sunshine and the protection of encircling hills. The wide,
man-made beach (with sand from the Sahara desert)
shelves gently into the sea, making this a popular destination for families with small children. The western arm of
the beach turns into a port, busy with offers of deep-sea-
fishing, sailing, diving, windsurfing, jet-ski-ing and
parascending trips. There are similar offers at Puerto Rico's
second port, the Puerto Nuevo, reached by a small bridge
over a creek at the eastern end of the beach.

Puerto Rico boasts a rarity among southern resorts: a
town park, planted with ficus trees and palms, behind the
beach. There is also a heated swimming pool, a bowling-
alley, flood-lit tennis, *fronton* (the Spanish alternative to
'fives') and mini-golf courts, a water park and a *centro
comercial* full of cheap shops and fast-food restaurants.

*The marina at Puerto
Rico, well-known for
water sports*

A Drive Around the South

This drive takes you from the coast to the central highlands through one barranco, and back down another.

Take the coast road to Arguineguín (➤ 42). At the roundabout behind the cement factory, turn right under the motorway for Cercado de Espina. Continue north into the barranco. At Cercado de Espina (12km), take the slip road right through the village. Soon, a steep zigzag climb begins, with wonderful views. At El Baranquillo Andrés (6km), a left turn is signed Mogán and Tejeda.

Another option is to continue onwards into Soria village, with its reservoir and restaurants, and turn right at Baranquillo Andrés to return to the route.

On the main route, turn left at Baranquillo Andrés. An asphalt road ascends through z-bends to meet the main (dirt) road ascending from Mogán. Turn right here for Tejeda.

The road soon runs close to a reservoir – Embalse de la Cueva de las Niñas – where there are agreeable picnic spots.

Continue 14km northeast through mountainous terrain for Ayacata. Turn right towards San Bartolomé de Tirajana; after 200m turn left (signed Los Pechos), climbing to pass Roque Nublo car-park. Continue through pinewoods, finally taking a right turn for Los Pechos, arriving at Pozo de las Nieves.

Again this part of the route offers fine views, as the ravine walls begin to narrow, of the great Roque Bermejo across the valley to the east.

Return to Ayacata and turn left to San Bartolomé. Follow signs for Fataga.

A hairpin descent takes you the into much-admired Barranco de Fataga, passing Fataga village and Arteara.

After a stiff climb out of the barranco, the road passes Mundo Aborigen (➤ 48) and continues to Playa del Inglés.

Distance
Approximately 115km

Time
About 5 hours' driving

Start point
Playa del Inglés
✠ 29D1

End point
Playa del Inglés
✠ 29D1

Lunch
Viuda de Viera (£)
✉ Cruce de Ayacata
☎ 928 12 73 94

+ 28D1

⊠ Municipality of San Bartolomé de Tirajana: 48km southwest of Las Palmas, 4km northeast of Playa del Inglés

Real Aero Club

⊠ Carretera General del Sur, km 46.5.

☎ 928 15 71 47

⏱ Daily by appointment. Closed Tue

💷 Expensive

❓ There is a weight limit of 91kg for participants

Gran Karting Club

⊠ Carretera General del Sur km 46

☎ 928 15 71 90

⏱ Daily, summer 11–10, winter 10–9

🍴 Café (£)

💷 Moderate

Above: grey, sandy beach at San Agustín

SAN AGUSTÍN ✪✪

Southern Gran Canaria's first shovelful of tourist concrete was laid in San Agustín. Curiously, this resort, a step away from popular Playa del Inglés (►54–5), has never been tarred with the brush of mass tourism. No doubt the presence of the 4-star Melia Tamarindos Hotel and its Casino have helped to maintain its up-market image.

The resort is cut in two by the 812 highway, leaving the hillside half connected to the beachside half by a series of bridges. The main beach, the dark-sand Playa de San Agustín, has the small Playa del Morro Besudo to its east and Playa de las Burras to the west.

The three large hotels (including the Tamarindos), all in Calle de las Retamas, are known for their splendid gardens. Much of the other accommodation is in low-rise apartments. San Agustín has its share of good restaurants, though none are in the dismal *centro comercial*.

A short distance northeast of San Agustín, the **Real Aero Club de Gran Canaria** offers tandem parachute jumps over the Maspalomas dunes – a thrilling way to see the island. Flying lessons are also available here.

Half a kilometre from the Aero Club, at a suitably noisy juncture between the carretera and the motorway, is the **Gran Karting Club**. Its 1,200m of track for Go-Karts and Mini-Karts is the longest in Spain and its clientele is of all ages. There is a pleasant lounge, café and games room and a sunny terrace for spectators.

SAN NICOLÁS DE TOLENTINO ✪

Sometimes known as 'La Aldea' or 'The Village', San Nicolás de Tolentino is tomato town. In a broad and dusty valley, well-settled in pre-Hispanic days, plastic greenhouses spread out in all directions. Towards the end of the season, tomato surpluses are dumped on wasteground, making brilliant splashes of colour. The town itself is mostly residential, with a cluster of shops round the church square and its restored Canarian-style church.

SIOUX CITY ✪

In the dry Barranco de Aguila, to the northwest of San Agustín and 300m from the beach, Sioux City is a Wild West theme park which has been created in the remains of an old spaghetti-western-style film set. Contributing towards the one-horse-town atmosphere are re-created saloons, church, bank, prison, bar and a sheriff's office. An action-packed show includes such diversions as knife-throwing, lassooing, pistol-shooting and, naturally enough, a bank robbery.

VECINDARIO ✪

Vecindario is a workaday town which stretches interminably along the main coast road. It is a recent creation born of rural depopulation and the demands of the tourist industry. Once a small village in a tomato-growing area, its size and relative prosperity have earned it the label *la ciudad de los Mercedes* – 'Mercedes city'. Though Santa Lucía de Tirajana theoretically remains the chief town of the district, the municipal offices are now in Vecindario. Street markets in Plaza San Rafael and Era de Verdugo sell excellent local produce.

➕ 28B4
✉ Municipality of San Nicolás de Tolentino: 71km southwest of Las Palmas, 70km northwest of Playa del Inglés
🍴 Cafés in town (£–£££)
🚌 38
🔁 Puerto de la Aldea (➤ 56)

➕ 29D1
✉ Cañón del Aguila
☎ 928 76 25 73
🕐 Daily 10–5
🍴 Cafés on premises (££)
🚌 Salcai bus 29
💰 Moderate
❓ Shows 12, 1:30, 3, 4:30

➕ 229E2
✉ Municipality of Santa Lucía de Tirajana: 51km south of Las Palmas, 18km northeast of Playa del Inglés
🍴 Many cafés (£–£££)
🚌 52
🔁 San Agustín (➤ 62)

Heroic civic sculpture marks the growing status of Vecindario

63

Central
Gran Canaria

For those who love high mountains and volcanic landscapes, vast basalt columns rising solitary from rocky platforms, deep valleys, greenery, wild flowers in abundance – the centre has to be the place.

Pozo de las Nieves is the highest point, more a mountain rim than a peak, looking down over the southeast. The free-standing Roque Nublo, a vast trunk of stone, rises almost as high, and looks west and southwest. Mountain villages, many with inhabited caves as well as houses, are gently domestic in atmosphere, white in colour, ancient in appearance. There are forests of Canarian pine, sometimes streaming with lichen, and echoing with woodpeckers. There are rocky hillsides dense with cistus, lavender, broom and thyme. There are short paths, long trails, rough roads and asphalt roads. Above all, there is a lofty landscape, offering drama and surprise at every turn.

'This Canaria is a land of mountains, trees, springs, streams, water wherever you look, and sharp-fanged cliffs.'

MARIN DE CUBAS
Historia de las Siete Islas de Canaria (1694)

29D2
Municipality of San Bartolomé de Tirajana: 55km south of Las Palmas, 10km north of Playa del Inglés
Nearest café in Fataga (£)
18, 42, 51
Fataga (► 68)

Only the belfry indicates that this cave in Arteara is a church

28C4
Municipality of Artenara: 49km southwest of Las Palmas, 91km north of Playa del Inglés
Good restaurants in town (£–£££)
220
Tamadaba (► 72)
Fiesta de Santa María de la Cuevita, last Sunday in Aug: grand occasion with cycling competition and torchlit processions

28C3
Municipality of Tejeda: 42km southwest of Las Palmas, 35km north of Playa del Inglés
18

ARTEARA ✪✪

Most visitors become aware of this tiny, fertile village, set in the dramatically beautiful Barranco de Fataga, only when they come here on camel safari. In fact, the camel ride skirts round the village and by-passes one of the most interesting pre-Hispanic sites on the island: an ancient necropolis, containing hundreds of graves. Early Canarios used stone coffins, as well as caves, to bury their dead. Here, the stones lie in rubble spread over 2sq km of hillside at the southern end of the village.

ARTENARA ✪✪✪

Dominated by a statue of Christ, this pleasant town is the highest on the island (1,219m). Every window, balcony or turn of the road offers thrilling views – from its northern side towards the pinewoods of Tamadaba (► 72), and from its southern side across the wide valley in which the Roque Bentaiga (► 69) rises in solid splendour. The surrounding landscape is riddled with caves, some of them in continuous habitation since pre-Spanish times.

The biggest attraction here is the small, charming cave church, the Santuario de la Virgen de la Cuevita. The image of the Virgin and Child stands above an altar and pulpit hewn out of solid rock. A restaurant, La Silla (► 96), can be reached through a rocky tunnel bored right through the end of the ridge which the town straddles.

AYACATA ✪

This mountain village, which serves as a staging post on the way to the highest point of the island from the coast, boasts a couple of restaurants, souvenir shops and some tremendous views – particularly in early spring, when the entire mountainside is covered in soft, pale clouds of almond blossom.

This intricately carved stone cross marks the centre point of the island

CRUZ DE TEJEDA ✪

At 1,450m, this cross, set in a rather scruffy square full of postcard kiosks, marks the notional centre of the island. The adjacent parador, which has seen better days, was built as a hotel in 1938 to a traditional design by Néstor de la Torre – a white house with exposed stone coigning and green woodwork. Although it is now only a lunchtime restaurant, it is worth stepping on to the dining room terrace for the exceptional views, which take in Roque Nublo and Bentaiga. A shop in the parador sells Canarian handicraft.

✚ 28C4
✉ Municipality of Tejeda: 37km southwest of Las Palmas, 78km north of Playa del Inglés
🍴 Food stands and restaurant in area (£–££)
🚌 29
↔ Tejeda (► 73)

EMBALSE DE SORIA ✪✪

This reservoir, built in 1971 at the head of the Barranco de Arguineguín, is the largest on the island, supplying water to the southern tourist resorts. It is also a popular swimming and fishing lake, fringed with Canarian palms standing among *taginastes* and *tabaiba*. Walkers who have laboured up the barranco often stop at the Bar Casa Fernando in the small village above the dam for a glass of freshly squeezed papaya juice. The menu also offers local goat's cheese, potatoes in *mojo* sauce and goat stew.

The only thing that disturbs the general tranquillity is the weekend convoys of jeeps which climb past Soria to the next reservoir, the Embalse de la Cueva de las Niñas. To the east, the Chira reservoir completes a trio of artificial lakes in the centre.

✚ 28C3
✉ Municipality of Mogán: 87km south of Las Palmas, 35km northwest of Playa del Inglés
🍴 In village (£)
↔ Ayacata (► 66)

White walls and exposed stone create a typical piebald effect in this Fataga house

FATAGA ✪✪

This charming town of white houses with pink roofs, sitting on a knoll in its barranco, is much praised as an example of all that is loveliest in Canarian mountain villages – not least by its own inhabitants. They describe their home as *típico, pequeño, bonito* – 'traditional, small and pretty' – and themselves, with no false modesty, as *muy amables* – 'very kindly'. There is no arguing with any of that.

Fataga's reputation has spread and the village now has several bars and souvenir shops on either side of the main street. This is the thoroughfare connecting San Bartolomé de Tirajana in the centre and Playa del Inglés in the south. But the village itself, so neat, with cobbled alleyways, white houses, pink roofs and floral patios, and cocks crowing in clear, mountain air, seems timeless. It falls steeply into curved terraces like stacked plates and ends in a barranco floor bristling with palms. Above, the cliffs walls are made up of rocks like organ pipes.

The tiny church, planted around with shady trees, was built in 1880 and bears a plaque marking its centenary and commemorating those who built *tan magna obra* – 'such a great work'.

FORTALEZA GRANDE ✪✪

Rising from the valley floor on the west side of highway 815, to the south of Santa Lucía, this fortress-like rock formation was the scene, in April 1483, of the last resistance of the aboriginal people against their Spanish conquerors. The final nucleus of 600 men and over 1,000 women and children were urged to surrender by their former king, Tenesor Semidan, who had joined the Spanish side and been baptized as a Christian. Refusing to listen to him, many of his former comrades threw themselves off the cliffs, calling out the name of their god, Atis Tirma, as they fell to their deaths.

ROQUE BENTAIGA   ✪✪✪

This dramatic monolith, raised like a rugged forearm with clenched fist, surges up to 1,404m from its own rocky massif, set in a broad valley. Visible from many points in the west and centre of the island, it is accessible by (very wiggly) road. For the aboriginal inhabitants of the island it was a sacred place and a scene of sacrifices. Bentaiga also made a most effective fortress, playing an important role in the resistance against the Spaniards. Its defenders, under cover of darkness, finally retreated from here to Ansite, where they congregated for their last stand. About 2km along road 17.3 from the Bentaiga/El Espinillo turning, in the westward extension of the massif, is the Cueva del Rey, a large, man-made cave, once painted, with side-chambers and floor holes.

➕ 28C4

✉ Municipality of Tejeda: 46km southwest of Las Palmas, 35km north of Playa del Inglés

↔ Roque Nublo (► 70)

❓ Half an hour's climb from the parking area on track signed to Bentaiga off 17.3 road

Worn survivor of a greater mountain: Roque Bentaiga

The Roque Nublo stands sentinel over the small town of Tejeda

ROQUE NUBLO ✪✪✪

Though it is a little lower in altitude than the island's highest point at Pozo de las Nieves (1,803m compared to 1,949m), this spectacular basalt monolith dominates many views in the centre of Gran Canaria. It appears to be the final, irreducible core of a far higher volcanic mountain, formed about 3.5 million years ago, in the island's second great wave of volcanic activity, and long since peeled away by wind, water, snow and ice. One other, smaller rock, El Fraile, stands close to it. There is a footpath from the car-park to the rocky plateau from which the Roque Nublo rises, and a footpath right round the little massif (➤ 71).

SAN BARTOLOMÉ DE TIRAJANA ✪✪

A quiet, agricultural town on the lip of a crater (the Caldera de Tirajana), San Bartolomé is the administrative head of the municipality which controls the tourist complexes of San Agustín, Playa del Inglés and Maspalomas. Climb its steep and sober streets, wander in its quiet squares and you will find a world far removed from the parched beaches of the deep south: a pastoral landscape of orchards and cultivated terraces.

San Bartolomé de Tirajana is famous for its local liqueur, *guindilla*, distilled from the sour cherry, or *guinda*, and combined with rum and sugar. It is served in the Bar Martin, in the main Calle Reyes Catolicos.

A Walk Around Roque Nublo

This well-kept path makes a complete circuit of Roque Nublo and ascends to the plateau where it stands. It involves gentle descents and one stiffer climb, worth it for wonderful vistas, embracing deep valleys, glimpses of the ocean, the Bentaiga monolith and nearer rocky mountain crests.

Leave the car-park by a small paved area, to follow the ridge directly ahead.

Views of Ayacata open out to the left, and there are fine views from the right-hand side of the ridge.

Near a finger of rock, the path begins to hairpin up; some 75m before the rock the path divides. Follow right to make the circuit beneath Roque Nublo (left ascends directly to Nublo). The path now leads gently down (take care not to slip on pine needles) to the northwestern corner beneath Roque Nublo.

From here a ridge to the right leads to a castle-like rock outcrop (don't try to climb this), with surprising views of the valley and of Roque Bentaiga (add 20 minutes for the diversion).

Back on the main path, climb gently upwards, then more steeply.

There is a clear view of Roque Nublo from below, with the lesser rock, El Fraile, now in silhouette.

After 10 minutes, take a clear branch of the path left. Another 15 minutes of climbing brings you to a rocky ridge. Turn left here, with rough steps up to the rock plateau and the base of Roque Nublo. Return to the preliminary ridge and turn left and down, passing the point where the path first divided, and return to the car-park.

Distance
6.5km

Time
Two hours; two hours are added by starting and finishing the walk in Ayacata.

Start/end point
Car-park, 2km north of Ayacata, steeply up, on road signposted Los Pechos
✚ 28C3

Lunch
Viuda de Viera (£)
✉ Cruce Ayacata, opposite the main Ayacata bus-stop
☎ 928 12 73 94

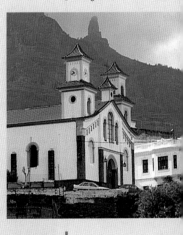

Tejeda church, with Roque Nublo in the background

71

SANTA LUCÍA ✪✪

Visitors come in coachloads to Santa Lucía's major attraction – its museum, Museo de la Fortaleza, in a former farmhouse now transformed into a pastiche of a miniature turreted castle. It contains an extraordinary jumble of old rocks, guns, stuffed birds, pressed flowers and amazing Guanche or pre-Spanish artefacts. These include pottery, tools, scraps of funerary clothes and other textiles made from reeds, astonishingly well-preserved, and a couple of skeletons. How such objects, part of the archaeological inheritance of the whole island, remain the property of a private individual – albeit a former mayor – is a puzzle. After the museum, visitors usually have lunch in the adjoining rustic-syle restaurant, El Hao.

Apart from these small diversions, which can create a traffic bottleneck, Santa Lucía is just another attractive mountain village presided over by its grand neo-classical church of white wall and dark grey stone. The business here is agriculture, particularly fruit-growing; the local liqueur is *mejunje*, made from lemons, rum and honey.

TAMADABA ✪✪✪

Eight kilometres from Artenara you will find the island's largest forest of Canary pines, much loved by walkers and picnickers, centred on the Pico de Tamadaba at 1,444m. There is a forestry station on the circular road leading round the mountain and an ICONA (national environmental agency) picnic site on the edge of the woods. There are splendid views from the summit down to the coast and, on a clear day, to Mount Teide on Tenerife.

The remains of a once extensive pine forest at Tamadaba

TEJEDA ✪✪

This peaceful and attractive mountain village is little visited because most people are *en route* to the tourist heart or centre of the island – the Cruz de Tejeda (➤ 67). Many young people have left Tejeda, once a thriving agricultural village, to find work in tourism-related industries; its major products now are sweets and cakes made from local almonds. At some point during the springtime, depending on the progress of the season, the town celebrates the Festival of Almond Blossom, Almendra en Flor, marking the beauty and commercial significance of the blossom.

TEMISAS ✪✪

Temisas is a village half-way up a mountainside, famous for its rural architecture – white stone houses with pink tiled roofs, windows with wooden shutters, a little 18th-century whitewashed church with a belfry, a water mill and hillsides dotted with olive trees (Temisas is sometimes known as 'Little Jerusalem'). Like many inland villages, though, the problem here is depopulation, with the young leaving for coastal towns in search of almost any work that is easier than tilling terraces.

From here there are clear views down to a coast of plastic greenhouses, with the town of Arinaga in the distance. The view is broken by the nearby bulk of a very solid rocky outcrop, unimaginatively named El Roque, rising from the plain beneath.

➕ 28C4
✉ Municipality of Tejeda: 37km southwest of Las Palmas, 78km north of Playa del Inglés
🍴 Bar in village (£)
🚌 29
↔ Cruz de Tejeda (➤ 67)

➕ 29D3
✉ Municipality of Agüimes: 35km south of Las Palmas, 33km north of Playa del Inglés
🍴 Bar in village (£)
🚌 34
↔ Fortaleza Grande (➤ 68–9)

Above: *tucked away deep in the interior, the charming agricultural village of Tejeda*

73

The North

Before the mushroom-growth of the southern resorts, the cloudier, rainier, greener and far more fertile north of Gran Canaria was the place to be. Both of the island's pre-Hispanic kingdoms had their centres here: one in Gáldar, in the northwest, the other at Telde, in the northeast. The Spanish capital of Las Palmas, in the northeast corner, became one of the leading cities of the Spanish nation. Behind Las Palmas, the hills are lushly suburban, but the landscape is surprising, interspersed as it is with volcanic craters and cones.

Inland towns and villages such as Teror, Gáldar and Arucas offer fine old Canarian architecture. Overwhelmingly, the main crop is bananas. Because of the general sense of fertility and greenery, the barrancos appear softened, and some – Agaete above all – produce fine tropical and subtropical fruits.

*'And often I forget
all life's uncertainties
thinking of these
islands, the mountains
beaches, waves.'*

NICOLAS ESTÉVANEZ
poet (1838–1914)

 28B5

Municipality of Agaete: 37km west of Las Palmas, 89km north of Playa del Inglés

2, 3

Puerto de las Nieves (► 83)

Fiesta de la Rama 4 Aug: a Christianised festival with strong aboriginal roots

Above: *the prosperous little town of Agaete, in the northwest*

AGAETE

Agaete stands at the mouth of the lush, green barranco of the same name. Its handsome old buildings, fanning out from a typical main square, with huge trees and a grand Canarian church, is one of the most charming spots on the island.

The church, the Iglesia de la Concepción, possesses a fine 16th-century Flemish triptych. This is shown during the Bajada de la Rama ('Bringing Down the Branch'), an ancient festivity celebrated in Agaete, Puerto de las Nieves (the town's little local harbour, 1km away) and in Puerto de la Aldea (► 56). On the lower side of town is a walled garden, the Huerto de las Flores, open to the public, venue for some of the town's cultural events. The 19th-century poet Tomás Morales wrote in these small and densely planted gardens.

The green and fruitful 7km-long Barranco de Agaete – producing mangoes and papayas, avocados, figs and coffee – eases the spirit after the harshness of so much of the island's volcanic landscape. There is one substantial tourist development, with privately owned houses and apartments, on the northern side of the valley. Elsewhere, ancient-looking villages run down on spurs from the barranco or cling to the steep slopes.

From the head of the barranco, there are fine views down towards the sea and upwards to the great bluff of Tamadaba, where Canarian pine forests fringe the top of a precipice.

ARUCAS ✪✪

Arucas is a lively, populous town with one extraordinary feature – the needle-pointed, frilly neo-gothic Church of San Juan Bautista, so commanding in size and colour that it is often·mistakenly called a cathedral. Built in a local grey basalt – *piedra azul*, or 'blue stone' – it was begun in 1909 and completed in 1977. The same stone, produce of a local quarry, is used in many Canarian buildings in Calle León y Castillo and Rua Francisco Gourie. The streets are unusually wide and straight, the result of a town planner's efforts in the mid-19th century.

The sombre grey basalt church of San Juan Bautista dominates the town of Arucas

Arucas used to be known as *la villa de las flores*, 'the town of flowers', and has fine subtropical gardens in the Municipal Park. Most of the greenery surrounding the modern town, however, is that of banana plantations, giving rise to a new description of Arucas: *republica bananera*, 'banana republic'.

Sugar cane and, even more so, the rum made from it, are also famous local products. An old-established distillery just beneath the town on the north side produces 50,000 litres of rum a day under the label *Arehucas* – the old Guanche name for the town. The distillery and the **Museo del Ron** (Rum Museum) are both open for visits by coach parties.

To the northeast of town, the great volcanic cone of Montana de Arucas – scene of the death of the last great aboriginal freedom fighter, Doramas, in 1481 – offers views of La Isleta and the Bay of Las Palmas.

✚ 29D5

⊠ Municipality of Arucas: 18km west of Las Palmas, 70km north of Playa del Inglés. Museo Ron Arehucas: Era de San Pedro, 2

🍴 Cafés in town (£–££)

🚌 205, 206

🔄 Firgas (➤ 79)

❓ Feast day of St John 24 Jun

Museo del Ron

☎ 928 60 00 50

🕐 Mon–Fri 10–2. Closed Sat–Sun

💷 Free

Did you know ?

Cock-fighting is a popular activity on the island and Arucas is famous for its cock breeders. The fighting season runs from February to April.

Above: *tracks lead down
to the farm at the bottom
of Bandama crater*

CALDERA DE BANDAMA ✪✪✪

The *caldera* or crater of Bandama forms a perfect bowl, 1km across and 200m deep, with no way out at the bottom. Its steep but gentle-seeming slopes are made up of dark grey ash, but the floor of the crater is patchily fertile, containing a single farm with chickens and goats, figs, oranges, palms and potatoes. The farmer, Juan, is something of a celebrity. You can walk down into the crater (about one hour) from the tiny hamlet of Bandama, taking a path past the church. Take care, though, as the steps soon peter out. Bandama, named after Dutchman Daniel van Damm, who arrived in 1560 and planted vines here, has a small bar which serves excellent roast pork and red wine.

There are superb views from the immediately adjacent Pico de Bandama *mirador* (574m), the peak itself being a large pimple on the volcanic rim. The *mirador* is popular with coach parties during the day and courting couples at night, with some resulting wear to the crater's upper slopes.

On the seaward side, there are lofty views over the two Tafiras and to Las Palmas. On the west side of the crater is the Club de Golf Bandama, the oldest golf club in Spain, founded in 1891 by the British community who settled in Santa Brígida and the neighbouring Tafiras. The club moved from Las Palmas to this marvellous site on the edge of the crater in 1956. The accompanying Hotel Golf Bandama, comfortable but seriously sporty, is owned by a naturalised Spanish Swede and patronised mostly by Scandinavians, Japanese and the local upper classes.

CENOBIO DE VALERÓN (➤ 19, TOP TEN)

CUATRO PUERTAS ✪✪
Cuatro Puertas (Four Doors) was a major religious site, used for worship and sacrifice by the aboriginal people of northeastern Gran Canaria. It comprises four cave openings, leading into a single large chamber. An open space in front was presumably ceremonial. The site is close to the summit of a windy hill, Montaña de Cuatro Puertas. From here, you see that the whole hill is part of the otherwise vanished rim of a volcano.

🕂 29E3
✉ Municipality of Telde: 19km south of Las Palmas, 35km northeast of Playa del Inglés
🍴 None on site; bar in village below (£)
🚌 36
🎟 Free

CUEVAS DE LAS CRUCES ✪
Five kilometres north of Agaete on the Gáldar road, Cuevas de las Cruces consists of a number of adjoining rock chambers originally inhabited by the Guanches, one with a chimney. Nowadays, they contain a good deal of litter. The corner is awkward – take care entering and especially leaving the car-park in front of the little complex.

🕂 28C5
✉ Municipality of Gáldar: 34km west of Las Palmas, 86km northwest of Playa del Inglés
🚌 105
🎟 Free

FIRGAS ✪
Pleasant little upland Firgas, 'capital' of the smallest municipality in Gran Canaria, is famous throughout the archipelago for its natural spring water: the bottling plant 5km out of town bottles 250,000 litres a day. In the town, whitewashed houses stand round a circular grey fountain. Firgas is also an agricultural community, producing bananas, cereals, fruit, watercress and yams.

🕂 29D5
✉ Municipality of Firgas: 25km west of Las Palmas, 78km north of Playa del Inglés
🚌 201

A cool seat in Firgas

Interior of the church of Santiago de los Caballeros in Gáldar

🞧 28C5
✉ Municipality of Gáldar:
27km west of Las
Palmas, 79km northwest
of Playa del Inglés
🍴 Bar in market (£), Café
Alcori (££) – both on Calle
Capitán Guesada
🚌 103, 105
↔ Santa María de Guía
(► 85)

GÁLDAR ✪✪

The most historic of all Guanche towns and now the centre of a banana growing area, Gáldar shelters from the sea behind the near-perfect volcanic cone of La Montaña de Gáldar. It has an excellent covered market (famous for handicraft and local produce) in the main street and a fine square, Plaza de Santiago. The church, with its wide neo-classical façade unusually built in a pale fawn-coloured stone, stands on the site of the palace of the former Guanche kings. The town also boasts a monument to Tenesor Semidan, the last king of Gáldar (Calle Guariragua), unveiled by King Juan Carlos I of Spain in 1986. The one-storey town hall on the corner of the square is a building of real charm in the best Canarian Hispanic-style. A dragon tree, planted in the patio in 1718, practically bursts through the walls.

A road runs out of the square for 200m, soon descending to an archaeological park, still under construction. This contains the famous Cueva Pintada (Painted Cave) of Guanche times (a model can be seen in the Museo Canario, Las Palmas: ► 33). Discovered by chance in 1873, it is elaborately decorated with squares, circles and triangles in red, black and white. The cave was closed to the public in the 1970s and remains so while work continues.

Did you know ?

Early Canarios worshipped the sun, which they called Alcora, or Alcorac, kneeling to face it at daybreak.

LA ATALAYA ✪✪

This once entirely trogloditic village 5km west of Santa Brígida (➤ 84) now has its fair share of free-standing buildings. But it continues to produce the kind of hand-made pottery first made by the aboriginal Canarios, without the use of the wheel and unglazed. They are sold by individual craftspeople from their cave workshops at the edge of the village. La Atalaya and the villages of Hoya de Pineda and Lugarejo are the main centres of pottery handicraft.

🞧 29E4
✉ Municipality of Santa Brígida: 12km south of Las Palmas, 52km north of Playa del Inglés
🚌 311
↔ Caldera de Bandama (➤ 78)

LA GUANCHA ✪✪

On an arid site behind the sparkling sea, hemmed in by village houses and banana plantations, substantial remains of pre-Hispanic dwelling places and communal tombs survive. In the larger tombs, a central shaft is surrounded by two rows of radial chambers, all of it encircled by a final wall – like chapels lining the apse in a Christian cathedral. Forty-three people were buried in the largest.

🞧 28C6
✉ Municipality of Gáldar: 29km west of Las Palmas, 81km northwest of Playa del Inglés
🍴 Bar in El Agujero (£)
🎟 Free
↔ Gáldar (➤ 80)

LOS BERRAZALES ✪✪

Set at the upper end of the Barranco de Agaete, Los Berrazales used to be a spa. An old fashioned spa hotel, La Guayarmina, still has guests but their activities are somewhat restricted now that the water is all bottled under the name Cumbres de Gáldar. Los Berrazales marks the start of the trail ascending inland to the high centre of the island and down to the north coast. Once it was busy with donkey traffic, grain moving one way and ground *gofio* the other. But the reservoirs above now retain all the water and the water-mills are in ruins.

🞧 28C5
✉ Municipality of Agaete: 42km southwest of Las Palmas, 89km northwest of Playa del Inglés
🍴 Casa Romántica, Valle de Agaete (££), Hotel La Guayarmina (££)
🚌 102

Los Berrazales

29D5

✉ Municipality of Moya:
34km southwest of Las
Palmas, 87km north of
Playa del Inglés

❓ On minor road off 150
Moya-Guía road, 3km
from Moya

LOS TILOS ✪✪

The name refers to the surviving one per cent of Gran
Canaria's original and ancient *laurasilva* (laurel) forest, still
holding on here under rigorous protection. You may survey
it from the very narrow road that runs through it but you
are not allowed to wander in it. This is a tiny nature
reserve, only about 200m long, made up of dense
evergreen and varied species climbing up almost vertical
banks from the stream bed.

29D5

✉ Municipality of Moya:
31km west of Las
Palmas, 90km north of
Playa del Inglés

🍴 Cafés in town (£–£££)

🚌 123

↔ Los Tilos (➤ above)

Casa Museo

✉ Plaza de Tomás Morales 1

☎ 928 62 02 17

🕐 Mon–Fri 9–2, 4–8, Sat
10–2, 5–9, Sun 10–2

✋ Free

Above: *the dramatically
situated church at Moya*

82

MOYA ✪✪

Seen from the west Moya is an astonishing place, with a
huge church, Nuestra Señora de la Candelaria, perched on
the very lip of a deep ravine. Small wonder that earlier
churches on the same site collapsed into the barranco: the
first in 1671, the next in 1704. A 15th-century image of the
Virgin was preserved, however, and the town remains
devoted to it. Moya has a delightful, lofty feel; the area set
on the east side of the church, safely separated from the
ravine, is well preserved. It includes the birthplace of the
poet and doctor, Tomás Morales (1885–1921), at No 1 in
the plaza now named after him – a fine, broad house with
balcony, now the **Casa Museo**. In prehistoric days, Moya
was home town of the future leader Doramas, a poor boy
who made good and moved to Telde when he became
guanarteme, only to die resisting Spanish conquest. The
town produces its own biscuits, *mimos* ('caresses') *de
Moya* and *suspiros* ('sighs').

PUERTO DE LAS NIEVES ✪✪

Puerto de las Nieves is the home port of Agaete, capital in turn of a rich agricultural area. For centuries, this was the only reasonable point of access to this part of the island. A ferry service from Tenerife carries day-trippers and their hire cars in both directions. One dark grey beach huddles under the cliff, looking south at the Dedo de Dios (Finger of God), a slender monolith left standing when the rest of the cliff was eroded. Next comes the harbour and a promenade, the Paseo de las Poetas.

The 16th-century Ermita de la Virgen de las Nieves (Hermitage of the Virgin of the Snows) houses the central panel of the triptych of the Virgin and Child by the Flemish painter Joos van Cleve (1485–1540). The side panels, showing St Francis of Assisi and St Antony of Padua, are displayed in the church in Agaete (▶ 76). The panels are put together during the Bajada de la Rama fiesta, when the two villages get together to share the fun.

➕ 28B5
✉ Municipality of Agaete: 39km west of Las Palmas, 91km northwest of Playa del Inglés
🍴 Fish restaurants on Paseo de las Poetas (£–£££)
🚌 101, 103
⛴ Daily ferries to Tenerife (2½-hour journey)

Puerto de las Nieves, with the Finger of God in the foreground

The Argus Monitor from New Guinea, now at home in Reptilandia Park

REPTILANDIA PARK

Set on the dusty slopes of an extinct volcano (Montaña Almagro), this park breeds and displays reptiles and amphibians. Snakes from all over the world, many of them deadly, are housed in glass cases, all identified by scientific and common name (in English and in German) and place of origin.

In addition to the three indoor exhibition rooms, there are large outoor terrariums of crocodiles, alligators, turtles, tortoises, lizards and frogs. These have been designed – with waist-high walls and a roof net – to allow the animals maximum protection in a natural-looking habitat which is also easily accessible to spectators. The owner is British zoologist Jim Pether.

SANTA BRÍGIDA

This comfortable, bourgeois town is so well connected by fast road to Las Palmas, that it is now virtually a suburb of the capital city – and definitely well-heeled. Despite white-washed houses and Canarian balconies, Santa Brígida has less of a Spanish feel to it than any other town on the island. Its wide, tree-lined streets and large villas set in spacious gardens owe much to early British settlers, many of them involved in the wine, then the banana business. Though often working in the city, they made their homes here, attracted by the town's altitude and cooler temperatures. Santa Brígida and its neighbourhood are noted for their excellent restaurants (➤ 97–8).

SANTA MARÍA DE GUÍA ✪✪

Usually known simply as Guía, this town is situated 3km east of its neighbour and friendly rival, Gáldar. As in Gáldar, it pays to leave the main road and enter the old quarter, climbing briefly if steeply up narrow but stately streets (start where the road makes an awkward bend). The Las Palmas to Gálda highway bypasses Guía and has restored the town to its early serenity.

Among the early settlers of Guía were Genoese bankers and merchants, so the town has the benefit of some fine architecture, such as the 16th-century Casa Quintana. As usual, the centrepiece is an old-fashioned main square with trees and a church (Santa María) in stern volcanic grey and white – in this case, however, with a floridly neo-classical façade designed by José Luján Pérez, Canarian sculptor–architect and native son of Guía. Begun in 1607, and mixing baroque with neo-classical, the interior of Santa María is colonial in feeling. The elegant town hall, in Canarian style, is also in the square. Guía is well known for craft – basketwork, carved-handled knives – but its most famous product is *queso de flor* ('flower-cheese'), made of goat's milk flavoured with artichoke flowers, best bought in the establishment belonging to Sr Santiago Giol, at Calle Marqués del Muni 34. This is a great barn of a shop, with cheeses laid out on bamboo mats, old photos of cheeses and cheese-makers, and wine bottles stacked all the way up the walls. There is no question of buying anything without first tasting it.

🚻 28C5
✉ Municipality of Santa María de Guía: 24km west of Las Palmas, 76km northwest of Playa del Inglés
🍴 Cafés in town (£–£££)
🚌 1, 2, 3
🔁 Cenobio de Valerón (► 19)

Below: *a parishioner at the doors of Santa María church in Guía*

Did you know?

The French composer, Camille Saint-Saëns, stayed and composed in Guía. Some of his works were first performed on the organ in the Church of Santa María

SARDINA

This is a little town of modern appearance right in the northwestern corner of the island. It faces south with views over the white-crested sea and along the coastline, with its magnificent cliffs. The town boasts some cave dwellings, cave boathouses and, as often, a cave restaurant. One is called, simply, La Cueva (➤ 98), tucked in where the road rounds the small but pleasing grey sand beach.

🕂 28B6
⊠ Municipality of Gáldar: 33km west of Las Palmas, 85km northwest of Playa del Inglés
🍴 Cafes in town (£–£££)
↔ Gáldar (➤ 80)

TAFIRA ALTA Y BAJA

Like their neighbour, Santa Brígida (➤ 84), the towns of Tafira Alta and Baja are now no more than comfortable residential suburbs of Las Palmas. They have large houses, ample gardens, and enjoy the proximity of the Jardín Canario (➤ 22) and the university campus. All is gracious suburban semi-rurality, spoiled only by the proximity of the busy 811 which runs through here from Las Palmas to Vega de San Mateo (➤ 90), passing through a narrow canyon of main street.

🕂 29E5
⊠ Municipality of Las Palmas: 8km south of Las Palmas, 53km northeast of Playa del Inglés
🍴 Cafés in both towns (£–£££)
🚌 301, 302
↔ Jardín Canario (➤ 22)

Light and shade on a wall in Tafira Baja, suburb of Las Palmas

Again like Santa Brígida, the area is known for good food (➤ 96–9). The Jardín Canario has an excellent restaurant and superb views by its top entrance. At the lower level, you can eat well in the village of La Calzada. The name of caves in the nearby barranco, Cuevas de los Frailes, recalls evangelising friars who were murdered by resistant Guanches. These same friars are immortalised in the name of a hotel, Los Frailes, built by an Englishman at the end of the 19th century, now a private house on the road above the Jardín Canario. Nearby Monte Lentiscal and Monte Coello are regarded as the best wine-producing area in the island.

TELDE ✪✪

Telde, in the east of the island and south of Las Palmas, is Gran Canaria's second largest town. Historically, it was the seat of the aboriginal king, or *guanarteme*, who controlled the eastern part of the island. Its environs are not inviting. Warehouses, factories and packing plants stretch down a dry and scrubby plain to the coastal motorway. The modern town centre is busy and thrumming with traffic. The old town centre, as anywhere on the island, is the best bit.

The most picturesque part is the *barrio* of San Francisco – a place of stone-coigned white houses, wooden balconies and pitched roofs around the 18th-century Church of San Francisco, home to rich merchants in earlier days. The major church, though, is San Juan Bautista (St John the Baptist), surrounded by cobbled streets and a pleasant square in the north of the town. It was begun early in the 16th century and finished in this century. Inside, above the ornate gilt *retablo*, is a life-sized figure of Christ sculpted from crushed maize, and weighing only some 5kg. It was made by Mexican Indians and indicates the amount of two-way traffic between the New World and the Canary Islands.

Telde is also the birthplace of the engineer who built the harbour at Las Palmas in 1882, Juan de León y Castillo. His former home is now a museum, the **Casa Museo León y Castillo**.

✚ 29E4
✉ Municipality of Telde: 21km south of Las Palmas, 77km northeast of Playa del Inglés
🚌 12, 80
🔄 Cuatro Puertas (➤ 79)

Casa Museo León y Castillo

✉ Calle León y Castillo 43–5
☎ 928 69 13 77
🕐 Mon–Fri 9–1
🍴 Near museum (£–££)
✋ Free

Above: *the bust of León y Castillo, the 19th-century engineer, outside his home, now a museum, in Telde*

+ 29D5

✉ Municipality of Teror:
21km southwest of Las
Palmas, 77km north of
Playa del Inglés

🚌 22, 25

↔ Vega de San Mateo
(► 90)

❓ Town and island fiesta,
Nuestra Senora del Pino,
8 Sep

**Casa Museo de los Patrones
de la Virgen**

✉ Plaza del Pino, 8

☎ 928 63 02 39

🕐 Daily when owners not in
residence, 10–5

🍴 Near museum (£–££)

♿ Moderate, free for
children under 10

Above: *a stone bench in
the quiet Plaza Teresa de
Bolívar, Teror*

TEROR ✪✪✪

Surrounded by green hills, the inland town of Teror is the island's greatest architectural gem, surviving unblemished in fine old Canarian style. One side of the imposing central square contains the basilica of Nuestra Señora de los Pinos, the church of our Lady of the Pines, patron saint of the whole island. The other three sides of the square (and the complex of buildings behind the basilica), represent the best of manorial Canarian building.

The **Casa Museo de los Patrones de la Virgen** is a 17th-century mansion open as a museum when the owners are not in residence. Furnished rooms around a beautiful patio, particularly the domestic accommodation such as bedrooms and kitchen, are fascinating.

A small, irregularly shaped square leading off the Plaza del Pino is dedicated to Teresa de Bolívar, born in Teror. Her son was Simón Bolívar, the South American revolutionary hero. The country of Bolivia bears his name.

Time your visit for a Sunday morning, when a lively market for general and local goods takes place behind the church. Look out for specialities like marzipan cakes made by Cistercian nuns, varieties of bread, cheese and sausages – particularly the *chorizo rojo*, the red sausage of Teror (with a soft consistency, like a paste).

A Drive From Las Palmas

This drive sets off from the capital towards the mountainous centre of the island and returns through the agricultural village of Vega de San Mateo (➤ 90) and the prosperous villa town of Santa Brígida (➤ 84).

From Las Palmas pick up the 813 at the city's edge through Tamaraceite. Follow signs for Teror and Arucas and at the road division, take the left to Teror.

This is the beginning of rurality. If you are exploring Teror, park behind the church.

Leave the town , and turn right after 1km on the Valleseco road, steadily climbing a road lined with eucalyptus. After 8km, you reach the look-out point, Mirador de Zamora.

High views look back over the town of Teror, and the large Restaurante Balcón Zamora does a brisk trade with coach parties.

After 2km, turn left to Artenara.

Soon you are up among pine woods, which give way to open hillsides of volcanic ash. Mirador de los Pinos de Gáldar offers views of whole north coast, from the fishing village of Sardina (➤ 86) to Las Palmas.

From Artenara either continue to Tamadaba pine forest (another 7km) or leave on the road to Tejeda.

The Tejeda road follows the mountainside, with views to the west of Roque Bentaiga (➤ 69) and Roque Nublo (➤ 70).

Stop in Tejeda; return on 811 to Cruz de Tejeda, centre point of the island (➤ 67). From Cruz de Tejeda, continue on 811 to Vega de San Mateo. Pass Santa Brígida and Tafira Alta to join the motorway into Las Palmas.

Distance
103 km

Time
About 6–7 hours with minimal stops

Start/end point
Las Palmas
✚ 29E5

Lunch
Mesón la Silla (££)
✉ Camino de la Silla 7, Artenara
☎ 928 66 61 08

+ 29D4
- Municipality of Vega de
  San Mateo: 21km
  southwest of Las Palmas,
  61km north of Playa del
  Inglés
- 303
? Town fiesta, Romería de
  San Mateo, 21 Sep

Museo Cho Zacarías
- Avenida de Tinamar
- 928 66 06 27
- Mon–Sat 10–1. Closed
  Sun
- Restaurant 1–4, closed
  Mon (££–£££)
- Moderate

*Shopping for basketwork
in the Sunday morning
market at Vega de San
Mateo*

VEGA DE SAN MATEO

Vega means 'fertile plain', and this prosperous town,
usually known as San Mateo, certainly deserves that
description – except in its hilliness. Almond, chestnut and
fig trees cover these foothills of the Tejeda crater. Well-
worked, terraced plots produce an abundance of fruit and
vegetables. The best pears and peaches on the island
come from San Mateo.

Traffic jams on the main street indicate the popularity of
San Mateo's Sunday morning market. However, only
farming stalwarts rise early enough to catch the livestock
market, held at first light. The general market takes place
in two huge hangars on the south side of town. One
contains stalls offering all the abundance of the land – fruit
and vegetables, bread, dried fruit, nuts and bunches of
sweet-smelling herbs, cakes and biscuits from Moya,
cheeses from San Nicolás. A second hangar is an
emporium of cassettes, old-fashioned felt slippers, jeans,
football scarves and sunglasses. In between the two,
traders lay their pottery and basketwork out on the ground.

The town's church, containing the 17th-century statue
of San Mateo, is fittingly dedicated to the patron saint of
farmers and cattle breeders. It was rebuilt in the last
century with the addition of a bell donated by Cuban
émigrés, former residents of San Mateo.

The **Museo Cho Zacarías**, in a handsome, converted
farmhouse beside the main road, is a privately owned
museum of rural life, containing a display of farm imple-
ments, ceramics, furniture, toys and cooking utensils.

Where To...

Las Palmas

Prices
Prices are approximate, based on a three-course meal for one without drinks and service:

£ = 1,500 pesetas
££ = 1,500–3,000 pesetas
£££ = over 3,000 pesetas

Casa Carmelo (£££)
Excellent grilled meat and fish of your choice. Friendly atmosphere.
✉ Paseo de las Canteras 2
☎ 928 46 90 56 🕒 Lunch, dinner

Casa Julio (££)
A restaurant decorated in nautical style; naturally, offers fish and seafood as its speciality. The chef produces excellent roast and grilled meat, too, and Canarian dishes served with a selection of wine from all the islands.
✉ C/La Naval 132 ☎ 928 46 01 39 🕒 Lunch, dinner. Closed Sun

Casa Montesdeoca (£££)
An elegant dining room and patio restaurant set in a restored mansion. Excellent food, service and atmosphere. Highly recommended.
✉ C/ Montesdeoca 10 ☎ 928 33 34 66 🕒 Lunch, dinner. Closed Sun

Centro Vasco Aterpe Alai (£££)
Basque food – often regarded as the best in Spain – is the speciality here. Try the *merluza a la vasca*, hake in a green parsley sauce accompanied by *chacoli*, a white, slightly sparkling wine.
✉ Menedez y Pelayo 10 ☎ 928 24 18 29 🕒 Lunch, dinner. Closed Sun and Aug

Churchill (£££)
This old colonial house with attractive garden invokes the early days of British settlement. Excellent food and stylish atmosphere.
✉ C/León y Castillo 274 ☎ 928 24 85 87 🕒 Lunch, dinner. Closed Sun and lunch Aug

Don Quijote (££)
Don't expect Spanish food in this typically Spanish-named restaurant. The flavour here is international, specifically Belgian, with the emphasis on steak.
✉ C/Secretario Artiles ☎ 928 27 27 86 🕒 Lunch, dinner

El Amir (££)
Middle Eastern food – couscous, falafel – served in cheerful atmosphere.
✉ C/Olof Palme 36 ☎ 928 22 12 43 🕒 Lunch, dinner. Closed Mon

El Cerdo Que Rie (£)
Mostly grills. Moderate prices for good food, especially flambés and fondues.
✉ Paseo de las Canteras 31 ☎ None 🕒 Dinner only

El Corte Ingles (££)
The popular lunchtime restaurant in this prestigious department store serves excellent food from an international menu.
✉ Avda Mesa y Lopez 18 ☎ 928 27 26 00 🕒 Lunch. Closed Sun and hols

El Herreño (££)
Busy old-town restaurant; good selection of tapas. Speciality, roast pork and wines from island of El Hierro.
✉ C/Mendizábal 5–7 ☎ 928 31 05 13 🕒 Lunch and dinner

El Novillo Precoz (£££)
A popular, family-run steak restaurant. Beef is flown in from Uruguay three times a week.
✉ C/Portugal 9 ☎ 928 22 16 59 🕒 Lunch, dinner. Closed Mon

El Padrino (££)
Above the Puerto de la Luz in Las Coloradas, this popular restaurant serves excellent fish and seafood and typical Canarian dishes.
✉ C/Jesús Nazareno 1 ☎ 928 46 20 94 🕐 Lunch, dinner

El Pote (£££)
Galician food and wine is the speciality here, although Canarian dishes like potatoes in *mojo* sauce and rabbit stew are excellent.
✉ Pasaje Juan Manuel Durán 41 ☎ 928 27 80 58 🕐 Lunch, dinner. Closed Sun

Galileo Galilei (££)
Good Castilian roast meat, especially roast lamb, is the speciality in this popular restaurant.
✉ C/Galileo 4 ☎ 928 27 54 60 🕐 Lunch, dinner

Hamburgo (££)
International cuisine with a few German touches, in the Isleta area. Very popular.
✉ C/Mary Sánchez 54 ☎ 928 46 97 45 🕐 Lunch, dinner

Hesperides (£)
Simple, well-cooked food; good, cheerful service. The patron is from El Hierro and stocks Herreño country wines.
✉ C/Sagasta 63 ☎ 928 46 16 54 🕐 Lunch, dinner. Closed Tue

La Casita (£££)
On the edge of Parque Doramas, this restaurant, in two dining rooms and covered terrace, caters for the discerning bourgeoisie and offers an extensive wine list.
✉ C/León y Castillo 227 ☎ 928 23 46 99 🕐 Lunch, dinner. Closed Sun

La Pasta Real (££)
Italian cooking, excellent pasta and good variety of vegetarian dishes.
✉ C/Secretario Padilla 28 ☎ 928 26 22 67 🕐 Lunch, dinner

Le Français (£££)
Classic French dishes, country cooking and good desserts.
✉ C/Sargento Llagas 18 ☎ 928 26 67 62 🕐 Lunch, dinner. Closed Sun

Meson Condado (££)
An unpretentious, friendly restaurant with fish and seafood cooked in the Galician manner.
✉ C/Ferreras 22 ☎ 928 22 48 24 🕐 Lunch, Dinner

Presidente (£££)
This Japanese restaurant serves local fish in an oriental manner. Popular at lunchtimes with businessmen.
✉ C/Barcelona 13 ☎ 928 24 75 85 🕐 Lunch, dinner

Restaurante Indio (£)
Very simple surroundings, good Indian food.
✉ C/Albareda 55 ☎ None 🕐 Lunch, dinner. Closed Sat evening, Sun

Rías Bajas (£££)
A popular restaurant serving fish and seafood in Galician style with excellent wine from northwest Spain.
✉ C/Simón Bolívar 3 ☎ 928 27 13 16 🕐 Lunch, dinner. Closed Sun

Tenderete (£££)
One of the city's top restaurants, serving the best of Canarian food.
✉ C/León y Castillo 91 ☎ 928 24 69 57 🕐 Lunch, dinner

Wine
Wine is now produced in only one small area of the island – El Monte – about 10km south of Las Palmas. There have been efforts made recently to improve the quality of the wine, but most people agree that its charm lies in its rough-and-ready country taste.

93

The South

Fresh Fish
Most visitors are familiar with the Spanish dish *paella* – a mixture of baked rice and seafood – but it is not an island speciality. Fish restaurants here pride themselves on really fresh fish: try it grilled or baked.

Agüimes
Tagoror (££)
Praised as much for its location – high above the Guayadeque ravine – as for its food: strictly the best of Canarian. The Tagoror is an essential restaurant.

✉ **Montaña Las Tierras, 21, Guayadeque** ☎ **928 17 20 58**
🕐 **Lunch, dinner**

Arguineguín
Bar Cofradía de Pescadores (££)
This fishermen's co-operative serves fresh fish straight off the fishing boats in the harbour. A simple, neighbourhood restaurant with a far-reaching reputation among both locals and visitors. The blackboard menu also offers alternatives for meat-eaters. Seating inside and out.

✉ **Avda del Muelle s/n** ☎ **928 15 09 63** 🕐 **Lunch, dinner**

Puerto Atlantico (££)
Excellent Spanish and international food in elegant setting.

✉ **Carretera a Mogán, km 68** ☎ **928 73 52 27** 🕐 **Lunch, dinner**

Maspalomas/Playa del Inglés/San Agustín
Amaiur (£££)
This top restaurant serves superb food from the Spanish Basque region. Try the *lomo de merluza con almejas* – hake in clam sauce.

✉ **Avda Neckerman, Maspalomas** ☎ **928 76 44 14**
🕐 **Lunch, dinner. Closed Mon**

Chez Mario (££)
The cooking is Italian, the pasta is home-made and the atmosphere is both stylish and welcoming.

✉ **Playa del Aguila, San Agustín** ☎ **928 76 18 17**
🕐 **Dinner**

Chipi-Chipi (££)
Courteous service and good food, well presented at moderate cost, is the hallmark of this unpretentious little restaurant.

✉ **Avda Tirajana, Ed. Barbados 1, Playa del Inglés** ☎ **928 76 50 88** 🕐 **Lunch, dinner**

El Portalón (££)
An elegant restaurant, as successful in meat as in fish cookery with a good wine list.

✉ **Avda Tirajana 27, Playa del Inglés** ☎ **928 77 20 30**
🕐 **Lunch, dinner**

El Timple (££)
For good Canarian home-cooking, head across the motorway from Playa del Inglés to San Fernando. Good value, excellent service.

✉ **Edificio Roque Aguyro, C/Alejandro del Castillo** ☎ **928 76 38 73** 🕐 **Dinner. Closed Mon**

Gorbea (£££)
The restaurant of the Hotel Gloria Palace is open to non-residents for dinner. It offers stunning views from the ninth floor and excellent Basque cuisine with an emphasis on fish and seafood.

✉ **Las Margaritas, San Agustín** ☎ **928 76 83 00** 🕐 **Dinner only**

Guatiboa (£££)
A top Canarian restaurant, part of a top hotel – the Hotel Maspalomas Faro, just yards away from the beach – serves excellent food in sumptuous surroundings.

✉ **Plaza de Faro 1,**

Maspalomas ☎ 928 14 22 14
🕐 Dinner

La Toja (£££)
Excellent fish restaurant in two dining rooms in the centre of Playa del Inglés. *Caldo de pescado*, fish and vegetable soup, is delicious.
✉ Avda Tirajana 17, Playa del Inglés ☎ 928 76 11 96
🕐 Lunch, dinner

Las Cumbres (££)
Typically Spanish restaurant serves excellent roast lamb.
✉ Avda de Tirajana 9, Playa del Inglés ☎ 928 76 09 41
🕐 Lunch, dinner

Loopy's Tavern (££)
Grilled meat and pizzas and a lively atmosphere in a Swiss-chalet-type restaurant.
✉ Las Retamas 7, San Agustín ☎ 928 76 28 92 🕐 Lunch, dinner

Meson Viuda de Franco (££)
Said to be the oldest restaurant in these parts. Still enjoys a reputation for tasty tapas, as well as blow-out meals.
✉ Cruce Vda de Franco 10, San Fernando de Maspalomas ☎ 928 76 03 71 🕐 Lunch, dinner

Pepe El Breca 11 (£££)
On the Fataga road just beyond San Fernando, this is the place to eat classic Canarian dishes like *sancocho*.
✉ Carretera de Fataga, Maspalomas ☎ 928 77 26 37
🕐 Lunch, dinner. Closed Sun

Mogán
Cafeteria Pub Düsseldorf (££)
A north European experience of hamburgers, hot dogs, steak and pizza.
✉ C/General Franco ☎ 928 56 92 73 🕐 Lunch, dinner

Grill Acaymo (££)
Rustic décor combined with thrilling terrace views. Canarian food a speciality.
✉ El Tostador 14 ☎ 928 56 92 63 🕐 Lunch, dinner. Closed Mon

Puerto Mogán
El Cafetín (£££)
Attractive restaurant, serving Canarian country cooking.
✉ Plaza de la Puesta del Sol 1 ☎ 928 56 52 02 🕐 Lunch, dinner

El Faro (££)
A great location in a small 'lighthouse' at the end of the fishing harbour. Sip a drink or attack a grilled fish.
✉ Puerto de Mogán ☎ 928 56 53 73 🕐 Lunch, dinner

La Bodeguilla Juananá (££)
Restaurant plus deli serving and selling local food and handcraft.
✉ Puerto de Mogán ☎ 928 56 50 44 🕐 Lunch, dinner. Closed Mon

Tu Casa (££)
Fish is the speciality here. Try the *parrillada de pescado* – variety of grilled fish.
✉ Puerto de Mogán ☎ 928 56 50 78 🕐 Lunch, dinner. Closed Tue

Puerto Rico
Don Quijote (££)
International cuisine at low prices. Children's menu.
✉ Centro Comercial ☎ 928 56 09 01 🕐 Lunch, dinner. Closed Sun

Oliver (££)
On the corner of the first floor, look out over the park and choose from a small but good menu with a French touch.
✉ Centro Comercial ☎ 928 56 19 03 🕐 Dinner. Closed Tue

Sancocho
Sancocho is a favourite traditional meal on the island. It is the sort of meal served to the whole family for Sunday lunch, causing much smacking of lips and kissing of fingers – but it may be an acquired taste. It is a dish of salt *cherne*, like bass (the saltier the better), served with boiled potatoes and *gofio*, either as dumplings or to thicken the gravy.

Central Gran Canaria & the North

Meat Eaters

Canarians are great meat eaters; beef (*carne de vacca*), usually of excellent quality, is flown in from South America. Pork (*cerdo*), lamb (*cordero*) and kid (*cabrito*) are local products. So, too, is rabbit (*conejo*), most typically eaten as *conejo en salmorejo* – rabbit cooked in onion, red pepper and oregano, and served in a piquant sauce.

Agaete

Casa Nando (££)
A popular restaurant with the rare distinction of serving good *tapas*, too. Goat cheese and olives from the island are excellent.
⊠ C/Concepción 11, Agaete old town ☎ None 🍽 Lunch, dinner

Casa Pepe (££)
A cheerful, popular place to eat meat or fish. Good value.
⊠ C/Alcalde Armas Galván 5 ☎ 928 89 82 27 🍽 Lunch, dinner. Closed Wed

Casa Romántica (££)
A delightful hotel/restaurant which serves both inter-national and Spanish food using fresh produce.
⊠ Valle de Agaete, km 3.5 ☎ 928 89 80 84 🍽 Lunch, dinner

Los Papayeros (££)
Canarian country cooking, scented with herbs. Soups and stews are a house speciality.
⊠ Alcalde Armas Galván, 22 ☎ 928 89 80 46 🍽 Lunch, dinner. Closed Sun

Princesa Guayarmina (£££)
The restaurant of a former spa hotel, a little run-down but sweetly old-fashioned, serves Canarian food surrounded by splendid scenery.
⊠ Valle de Agaete, km 7 ☎ 928 89 80 09 🍽 Lunch, dinner

Artenara

La Esquina (££)
Roast lamb is the speciality of this friendly restaurant with stunning views from a terrace *mirador*. Artenara is the highest village in Gran Canaria.
⊠ Plaza de San Matias ☎ None 🍽 Lunch, dinner

La Silla (££)
Traditional Canarian food and grills are served in this cave restaurant with tremendous mountain views.
⊠ Camino de la Silla 7 ☎ 928 65 81 08 🍽 Lunch

Arucas

La Barca (££)
Much praised fish and seafood restaurant in San Andrés, a fishing hamlet in the municipality of Arucas. Your choice depends on the day's catch.
⊠ Carretera del Norte 26, San Andrés ☎ 928 62 60 88 🍽 Lunch, dinner. Closed Sun dinner

Mesón de la Montaña (£££)
Famous for its hilltop views, as well as its cooking and excellent wine cellar.
⊠ Montaña de Fuego s/n ☎ 928 60 14 75 🍽 Lunch, dinner

Rincón Canario (££)
A good place to try a *tapa* of local specialities – cheese or *chorizo*. Pleasant atmosphere.
⊠ C/ Arquitecto Vega 2 ☎ None 🍽 Open all day

Gáldar

Alcori Restaurante (££)
Cheerful, bustling, town-centre restaurant.
⊠ C/ Capitán Quesada ☎ 928 88 27 12 🍽 Lunch, dinner.

La Atalaya

El Castillete (££)
Select and cook your own meat at the barbecue or on a hot stone at your table. Very popular restaurant, with its rustic atmosphere. Book at weekends.
⊠ El Raso 7, La Atalya ☎ 928 35 24 43 🍽 Lunch, dinner

La Picota (££)

A family-run restaurant serving Spanish and Canarian specialities with the emphasis on fresh ingredients, simply prepared. Good home-made desserts.

✉ C/Cura Navarro 42, La Atalaya ☎ 928 64 26 78 🕓 Lunch, dinner. Closed Sun dinner, Mon

Moya
Casa Placido (££)

An enchanting location, beside the church at Moya overlooking the ravine. Serves hearty local dishes. Try the goat stew.

✉ Simón Milián 5 ☎ None 🕓 Lunch. Closed Mon

La Costa (£££)

Fresh fish cooked well in pleasant, popular restaurant.

✉ Carretera la Costa km 14, Moya ☎ 928 62 03 80

Puerto de las Nieves
Capita (££)

Freshest fish, excellent service, in this bustling, cheerful restaurant.

✉ Puerto de las Nieves 37 ☎ 928 55 41 42 🕓 Lunch, dinner

El Dedo de Dios (£££)

Seafood soup and fish stew with *gofio* is the speciality here – Canarian fish cooking at its best.

✉ Puerto de las Nieves ☎ 928 89 80 00 🕓 Lunch, dinner

El Puerto de Laguete (££)

Crowded at weekends and never empty during the week, this fish restaurant is famous for its food and its atmosphere.

✉ Nuestra Señora de las Nieves 9 ☎ 928 55 40 01 🕓 Lunch, dinner. Closed Mon

Las Nasas (£££)

A superb fish restaurant in an area renowned for fish restaurants. Terrace to the beach.

✉ C/Puerto de las Nieves ☎ 928 55 41 94 🕓 Lunch, dinner

Santa Brígida
Bentayga (£££)

First-class restaurant which uses the best of local produce in local cuisine. Meat dishes, particularly lamb and goat, are highly recommended.

✉ Carretera del Centro 130, Monte Coello ☎ 928 35 02 45 🕓 Lunch, dinner

Cafetería Churrería Mall (£)

The best place in Santa Brígida for breakfast, especially if you like *churros*, deep-fried dough rings.

✉ C/José Antonio Primo de Rivera, near the Post Office ☎ None 🕓 Open all day

Casa Martel (£££)

Old-fashioned country restaurant which is equipped with an excellent wine cellar.

✉ Carretera del Centro, km 18, El Madroñal ☎ 928 64 12 83 🕓 Lunch, dinner

Grutas de Artiles (£££)

This establishment enjoys a well-deserved reputation for serving good Spanish food in a lively setting which includes a garden, tennis courts, swimming pool and caves.

✉ Las Meleguiñas, Santa Brígida ☎ 928 64 05 75 🕓 Lunch, dinner

Los Geranios (£)

Famous for roast and grilled pork and local red wine, this simple village bar is crowded at weekends.

✉ Barrio de Bandama ☎ None 🕓 Lunch, dinner

Mano de Hierro (££)

A family-run German restaurant offering *eisbein* and *sauerkraut* and Spanish favourites such as *chorizos*.

✉ El Pino 25, Santa Brígida ☎ 928 64 03 88 🕓 Lunch, dinner. Closed Mon

Fish

Even on an island, demand for fish (*pescado*) can often outstrip supply. Beware of thawed frozen fish sold as fresh. Good, fresh fish is expensive, even if it is bought straight out of the fisherman's nets. Tuna, cod, hake, swordfish, mackerel and sardines are familiar to everyone and are available on most menus. Try the local varieties like *cherne* (similar to bass), *sama* (like sea bream) and, a speciality in Gran Canaria, *vieja* (like parrotfish).

97

Central Gran Canaria & the North

Canarian Beer
Most Canarios drink beer, *cerveza*, with their food. A small glass of beer is a *caña*. *Tropical* is the major island brand, but *Dorada* from Tenerife is also popular. All international brands are available on the island.

Pizzería California (££)
Tasty pizzas, light meals and sandwiches in a cheerful neighbourhood café.
✉ C/Manuel Hernández Muñoz 5 ☎ 928 64 27 03 ⏰ Lunch, dinner

Satautey-Hotel Escuela (££)
This restaurant of the Hotel Santa Brígida (a working hotel and a hotel training school) wins enthusiastic plaudits for the quality of food and service – a testimony to the professionalism of the catering students who are in charge of it.
✉ Real de Coello 2, Santa Brígida ☎ 928 35 55 11 ⏰ Lunch, dinner

Santa Lucia de Tirajana
Hao (££)
Country food is served at wooden tables and benches in this mountainside village. The restaurant is particularly popular with visitors to the neighbouring Museum of Canarian Life. Arrive before 12:30, or after 2, to avoid coach parties.
✉ C/Tomas Arroyo Cardosa ☎ 928 79 80 07 ⏰ Lunch

Santa María de Guía
Los Crotos (££)
Situated down on the coast in the municipality of Guía, this fish restaurant enjoys an island-wide reputation for its simple but excellent cooking.
✉ Carretera de San Felipe km 2, Guía ☎ 928 55 64 01 ⏰ Lunch, dinner. Closed Sun dinner

San Mateo
Cho Zacarías (££)
Good country cooking in an old farmhouse which has

been turned into a museum of rural life.
✉ Avda Tinamar ☎ 928 66 06 27 ⏰ Lunch. Closed Sun

El Secuestro 11 (££)
Another well-known San Mateo restaurant where you can enjoy *papas arrugadas* (potates cooked in their skins), *mojo* sauce and grilled meat.
✉ Avda Tinamar s/n ☎ 928 66 12 78 ⏰ Lunch, dinner

La Vaguetilla (£££)
This is an ideal restaurant in which to enjoy a long, slow Sunday lunch. Canarian and Spanish food, beautifully cooked and served. Eat in the restaurant or garden.
✉ Carretera del Centro km 20.300 ☎ 928 66 07 64 ⏰ Lunch, dinner. Closed Tue

Sardina del Norte
Fragata (£££)
A fish restaurant that looks like the inside of a frigate, right at the end of the harbour with lovely open views of the sea. Choose your own fish, lobster or crab.
✉ Muelle Nuovo, Puerto de Sardina ☎ 928 88 32 96 ⏰ Lunch, dinner. Closed Mon

La Cueva (££)
A small cave restaurant serving fresh fish, either in the cave or on the terrace outside. Simple but sweet.
✉ Playa de Sardina ☎ 928 88 02 36 ⏰ Lunch, dinner

Miguelín (££)
A simple fish restaurant. Each dish is freshly prepared and cooked to order. Excellent value.
✉ Carretera de Sardina, km 5, 79 ☎ 928 88 00 15 ⏰ Lunch, dinner. Closed Mon

Tafira

Casa Miranda (££)
Simple, neighbourhood restaurant serving well-cooked food in agreeable surroundings.
✉ **Camino Vecinal, C/Los Hoyos 90, Tafira Alta** ☎ **928 35 45 10** 🕐 **Lunch, dinner**

Jardín Canario (£££)
A wonderful setting on the edge of the cliff above the botanical gardens. The food is excellent Canarian, the service is elegant.
✉ **Carretera del Centro, km 7.200, Tafira Alta** ☎ **928 35 16 45** 🕐 **Lunch, dinner**

La Masia de Canarias (£££)
This country restaurant serves wholesome Canarian food from fresh local ingredients.
✉ **C/ Murillo 36, Tafira Alta** ☎ **928 35 01 20** 🕐 **Lunch, dinner**

Los Conejos (££)
Rabbit (*conejo*) – deliciously cooked in herbs – is the speciality of this popular restaurant.
✉ **La Calzada 18, (near the lower entrance to Jardín Canario)** ☎ **928 35 17 02** 🕐 **Lunch, dinner. Closed Tue**

Tejeda

Cueva de la Tea (££)
A good, unpretentious restaurant in Tejeda, specialising in roast meat.
✉ **C/Dr Hernández Guerra** ☎ **None** 🕐 **Lunch**

El Refugio (££)
In an incomparable situation among the high peaks of the island, this restaurant, popular with coach parties, offers a Spanish and international menu.
✉ **Cruz de Tejeda** ☎ **928 66 61 88** 🕐 **Lunch**

Telde

La Pardilla (££)
A couple of kilometres towards the coast northeast of Telde, this restaurant is highly praised for its traditional Canarian cuisine, particularly its *mojo* sauces to accompany charcoal-grilled meat. The *puchero canario* – a rich meat and vegetable stew – is another favourite.
✉ **C/Raimundo Lulio 54, La Pardilla** ☎ **928 69 51 02** 🕐 **Lunch, dinner**

Restaurant Bahía Mar (££)
Excellent restaurant of the Hotel Bahía Mar on the coast at Garita offers Canarian and international cuisine but prides itself on fish and seafood dishes.
✉ **Urbanización La Estrella, La Garita** ☎ **928 13 08 08** 🕐 **Lunch, dinner**

Teror

Balcón de la Zamora (££)
Fine views from the look-out point and excellent kid stew in this busy roadside restaurant.
✉ **Carretera a Valleseco km 8** ☎ **928 61 80 42** 🕐 **Lunch, dinner**

El Secuestro (££)
Very reasonable prices charged for ample portions of good home cooking, particularly roast meat. Full at weekends.
✉ **Avda Cabildo Insular s/n** ☎ **928 63 02 31** 🕐 **Lunch, dinner. Closed Mon**

Vegetarians

Vegetarians may feel sadly neglected in island restaurants despite the quality and variety of local vegetables. A meal consisting only of vegetables is a novel concept to most Canarian cooks, who will happily produce a vegetable stew full of beans, carrots, sweet potatoes and artichokes, then add a blood sausage or pork chop for supposed extra nutrition. Similarly, when you order a salad, it is worth mentioning if you do not want tuna (*atun*) or egg (*huevo*) added.

Las Palmas

Prices
Prices are for a double room, excluding breakfast and VAT:

£ = up to 6,000 pesetas
££ = 6,000–9,000 pesetas
£££ = 9,000 pesetas upwards

The rates vary enormously, depending on the season and the state of the local economy.

Capital Hotels
Although early tourists preferred the north of the island and made their base in Las Palmas, the choice of hotel accommodation in the capital is now rather limited in comparison with what is on offer in the southern resorts. In general, visitors who choose to stay in Las Palmas tend to be business travellers or those in flight from other tourists.

Alva (££)
Good, budget hotel in a busy part of town but close to the Canteras beach.
✉ Alfredo L Jones
☎ 928 26 42 28

Astoria (££)
A modern hotel near Playa de las Canteras with terrace, swimming pool, gym and squash courts.
✉ C/Fernándo Guanarteme 54
☎ 928 22 27 50

Cantur (££)
Comfortable, 1960s-built hotel with terrace; many rooms with view of Playa de las Canteras.
✉ C/Sagasta 28 ☎ 928 27 30 00

Colón Playa (££)
An apartment block situated at the beach end of this busy street. Go for the sea-view rooms.
✉ C/Alfredo Jones 45
☎ 928 26 59 54

Concorde (£££)
A modern hotel, comfortable and well-run, close to Canteras beach and Parque Santa Catalina. Swimming pool.
✉ Tomás Miller 85
☎ 928 26 27 50

Corinto (££)
Close to Canteras beach and the Parque Santa Catalina, this family-run hotel is clean and comfortable and has a coffee shop and bar.
✉ C/Prudencio Morales 41
☎ 928 46 89 74

Fataga (££)
A middle-range hotel in the business area of the city within easy walking distance of both Canteras and Alcaravaneras beaches.
✉ C/Nestor de la Torre 21

☎ 928 29 06 14

Faycan (£)
Moderately priced, clean and comfortable hotel in a central situation.
✉ C/Nicolas Estevanez 61
☎ 928 27 06 50

Hotel Madrid (£)
Built in 1910, and favoured by artists and intellectuals (General Franco stayed in room 3 in 1936) this family-run hotel is slowly being updated.
✉ Plaza de Cairasco 2
☎ 928 36 06 64

Hotel Parque (££)
Well situated for the old town, just across the road from the Parque San Telmo, this is an excellent middle-range hotel. Good bus service to southern resorts from nearby bus station.
✉ Muelle de las Palmas
☎ 928 36 80 00

Hotel Residencia Atlanta (£)
A modest hotel set in a central location close to Canteras Beach.
✉ C/Alfredo L Jones 37
☎ 928 26 50 62

Hotel Residencia Pujol (£)
A good budget hotel with easy access to the port and Canteras Beach.
✉ C/Salvador Cuyas 5
☎ 928 27 44 33

Hotel Residencia Tamadaba (£)
A simple budget hotel towards the south end of Canteras beach.
✉ C/Pelayo 1 ☎ 928 26 20 00

Imperial Playa (£££)
Pleasant, comfortable hotel on the north end of Canteras

beach, complete with satellite TV and air-conditioning. Excellent breakfast. Sauna and squash courts.

✉ C/Ferreras 1 ☎ 928 46 48 54

Majórica (£)
Right on Parque Santa Catalina and therefore likely to be noisy, this hotel is nevertheless clean and cheap.

✉ C/Ripoche 22 ☎ 928 26 28 78

Marsin Playa (££)
Comfortable apartments facing the beach at Las Canteras. It is worth paying out a little extra to get the sea views.

✉ Luis Morote 54 ☎ 928 27 08 08

Meliá Las Palmas (£££)
Luxury hotel in the middle of Playa de las Canteras, with shops, disco and a swimming pool.

✉ C/Gomera 6s ☎ 928 26 76 00

Princesa Herminda (££)
Clean, well supervised apartments, many of them with a sea view.

✉ C/Kant 1 ☎ 928 26 29 68

Reina Isabel (£££)
Luxury hotel in an unrivalled position on the Canteras Beach, with a superb high-rise restaurant, Parrilla Reina Isabel, and a gym and swimming pool on the roof terrace.

✉ C/Alfredo L Jones 40, Las Palmas ☎ 928 26 01 00

Rocamar (£££)
Comfortable, modern hotel at the northern end of Canteras Beach. Good value.

C/Lanzarote 10 ☎ 928 26 56 00

Sansofé Palace (£££)
An excellent modern hotel

which occupies a fine position, near Canteras Beach.

✉ C/Portugal 68 ☎ 928 22 40 62

Santa Catalina (£££)
Gran Canaria's top city hotel in a quiet, shady park. Canarian architecture, fine restaurant – Restaurante Doramas – and a casino. Tennis and squash courts, swimming pool.

✉ León y Castillo 227, Parque Doramas ☎ 928 24 30 40

Sol Bardinos (££)
The circular tower of this hotel, equally accessible from Canteras Beach and the Parque Santa Catalina, dominates the city skyline. Formerly luxurious but now in need of renovation work, it still offers glorious views and has a swimming pool and a solarium.

✉ C/Eduardo Benot 5 ☎ 928 26 61 00

Sol Iberia (££)
With fine views of the Paseo Marítimo, this large, rather faded-looking hotel is nevertheless very comfortable.

✉ Avda Alcalde Ramírez Bethencourt 8 ☎ 928 36 11 33

Tenesoya (££)
This is more a business than a tourist hotel. The facilities are good and the service friendly and efficient.

✉ C/Sagasta 98 ☎ 928 46 96 08

Trocadero (££)
A well-run and extremely popular hotel conveniently close to the beach and town facilities.

✉ C/Los Martínez de Ezcobar 61 ☎ 928 27 07 00

Lateen Sailing
Lateen sailing is a sport peculiar to this island. Small boats with huge sails race around the Bay of Las Palmas between April and September. Watch them (Saturday afternoon and Sunday morning) from the Avenida Marítima in Las Palmas.

The South

For Tennis Fans

Tennis players – or would-be tennis players – in search of total immersion in the game should book into the Tennis Hotel (££) ✉ Barranco de los Palmitos (☎ 928 14 21 00) for six artificial grass courts, swimming pool, sauna and a sporty atmosphere. Not far from here, in Monte Leon, is an exclusive and well-hidden millionaire's enclave of sumptuous villas, the haunt of international celebrities (mostly musicians) and heads of state. No hotels, though.

Fataga

Molino de Fataga (££)

A small, rural hotel in the Fataga valley with offers of camel rides, hearty Canarian cooking and an old *gofio* mill.
✉ **Carretera Fataga a San Bartolome km 1** ☎ **928 17 20 89**

Maspalomas/Playa del Inglés/San Agustin

Costa Canaria (£££)

The hotel is large and rather unimaginatively solid, but the gardens are superb and these attract many returning guests.
✉ **Las Retamas 1, San Agustín** ☎ **928 76 02 04**

Dunamar (£££)

An incomparable position on the beach and the views from sea-facing rooms make this hotel special. Swimming pool, squash.
✉ **Avda de Helsinki 8, Playa del Inglés** ☎ **928 77 28 00**

Faro Maspalomas (£££)

Luxury hotel metres away from the lighthouse after which it is named. The sea views are glorious, the hotel restaurant Guatiboa is one of the best on the island and guests are entitled to a discount on the Maspalomas golf course green fees.
✉ **Plaza del Faro, Maspalomas** ☎ **928 14 22 14**

Gloria Palace (£££)

Large, well-established hotel in San Augustin with a new thalassotherapy (sea-water therapy) centre (☎ 928 77 64 04) adjacent which is open to non-residents.
✉ **Las Margaritas** ☎ **928 76 83 00**

Maspalomas Oasis (£££)

Undoubtedly the most luxurious hotel in the south, the Oasis is situated on the beach, beside the dunes and surrounded by palms.
✉ **Playa de Maspalomas** ☎ **928 14 14 48**

Meliá Tamarindos (£££)

Luxury hotel in a quiet situation with superb gardens; casino and cabaret on premises.
✉ **Las Retamas 3, San Agustin** ☎ **928 77 40 90**

Riu Palace Meloneras (£££)

The first building to go up on Meloneras *urbanizacion* is a grand, white-wedding-cake of a hotel, with apartment chalets on lawns around a pool. The complex includes a golf course, conference centre and shopping mall.
✉ **Playa Meloneras** ☎ **928 14 31 82.**

Patalavaca

Steigenberger (£££)

A luxury hotel, the only one of a famous German chain on Gran Canaria, with a beautiful garden and pool and amazing sea views. Tennis and squash.
✉ **Patalavaca** ☎ **928 15 04 00**

Puerto Mogán

Club de Mar (££)

The only hotel – the rest are apartments – in the resort; comfortable, with a pool, tennis court and restaurant.
✉ **Puerto Deportivo** ☎ **928 56 50 66**

Hotel Taurito Princess (£££)

A splendid hotel just above the beach in this small resort. Great views of garden, pool and coast.
✉ **Urbanización Taurito s/n** ☎ **928 56 55 10**

Central Gran Canaria & the North

Agaete

Casa Romántica (££)
This very successful restaurant has now opened its doors as a rural hotel. Idyllic setting, good food, excellent service.
✉ Valle de Agaete km 3.5
☎ 928 89 80 84

El Angosto (£)
Basic but comfortable apartments just at the entrance to the town of Agaete. Choose rooms with balcony and sea views.
✉ Camino al Angosto
☎ 928 55 41 92

Hotel Guayarmina (££)
An old-fashioned spa hotel in a green and fertile valley. Ideal for quiet walks in the countryside.
✉ Los Berrazales, Valle de Agaete ☎ 928 89 80 09

Agüimes

Villa de Agüimes (£)
A 19th-century house transformed into a charming, small rural hotel by the local council.
✉ C/ Sol 3 ☎ 928 12 41 83

Gáldar

Hotel Hacienda de Anzo (££)
An old traditional house turned into a simple country hotel, complete with pool and garden.
✉ Valle de Anzo
☎ 928 55 16 55

Moya

El Cortijo (£)
A small, deeply secluded hotel/restaurant set in a rural landscape – ideal for those seeking peace and quiet.
✉ Camino de Hoyas del Cavadero 11, Carretera Moya a Fontanales, km 21.3 ☎ 928 61 02 85

Santa Brígida

Hotel Golf de Bandama (££)
A small country house/golf hotel on the edge of the Bandama crater, just 15m from the first hole. Most rooms have views of the course and the pool.
✉ Bandama s/n
☎ 928 35 33 54

Hotel Santa Brígida (££)
In the cool hills of Monte Lentiscal, this hotel is now a training school as well as a fully functioning hotel with a splendid dining room, gardens and pool; it enjoys an excellent reputation.
✉ C/Real de Coello 2, Santa Brigida ☎ 928 35 55 11

Residencia Tiempo Libre (£)
This hotel, subsidised by the Canarian government, is the cheapest good quality accommodation available. Advance bookings (essential) are taken for a minimum of three days on a full board basis. Large rooms with own bath, excellent food.
✉ Camino a los Olivos 1
☎ 928 64 04 50

Tejeda

El Refugio (££)
A rural hotel with 10 double rooms decorated in Canarian style.
✉ Cruz de Tejeda s/n
☎ 928 66 65 13

Telde

Hotel Bahía Mar (££)
Right on the seafront in a quietly pleasant setting 6km from the Old Town. Tennis and squash courts, swimming pool and a restaurant.
✉ Urbanización La Estrella, La Garita ☎ 928 13 08 08

Getting Around
You can stay in Las Palmas and still enjoy a visit to the southern resorts by taking one of the buses run by SALCAI (green – ☎ 928 37 36 25/76 53 32). UTINSA (blue) operates in the centre and north of the island (☎ 928 36 01 79). The bus terminal is at Parque de San Telmo, Las Palmas.

103

Las Palmas

Opening Hours
Shops open from 10 to 1:30 or 2, and from 4:30 to 8. When they are shut, they are very shut: that is, boarded up, so even window shopping is impossible. The department store El Corte Ingles on Avenida Mesa y Lopez in Las Palmas is open all day. It holds enough stock to satisfy the most compulsive consumer, until everything else opens again after lunch.

The best places to shop in Las Palmas are the streets around the Parque Santa Catalina and in the Triana district, particularly the pedestrianised Calle Mayor de Triana and the small streets off it.

Books

La Librería
The best bookshop in Las Palmas is run by the island government and stocks a wide range, including interesting material about Gran Canaria, books on flora and fauna and guide books. El Corte Inglés (see below) also has a good book section.
✉ C/Cano 24 ☎ 928 38 15 39

Department Stores

El Corte Inglés
The only large department store on the island is on both sides of the street. You can buy anything from local cheeses to perfume, clothes and furniture. Marks & Spencer have a branch at No 34 and in the Old Town in Calle Mayor de Triana 1.
✉ Avda Mesa y Lopez 18
☎ 928 27 54 08

Electronic Goods

Maya
A reputable chain of retailers dealing in cameras, videos, TVs, mobile phones etc.
✉ Calle Mayor de Triana 107
☎ 928 37 20 49

Visanta
Do not try to bargain at this well-established electronic store. Prices are fixed and goods are guaranteed. There is another branch on C/29 de Abril and in the Yumbo

Centrum, Playa del Inglés.
✉ C/Ripoche 25 ☎ 928 27 17 14

Fashion

Blas
A good choice for jeans, particularly well-known brands such as Levis.
✉ C/Tomás Miller, 67 and C/Ripoche 21

Boutique Gema
Modern clothes for young women.
✉ C/Travieso

Gucci
Smart Canarios favour Italian fashion, particularly Gucci accessories.
✉ C/ Viera y Clavijo 6
☎ 928 36 09 80

Nina Ricci
Italian designer fashion.
✉ Presidente Alvear 12
☎ 928 29 05 48

Zara
High fashion geared to young tastes.
✉ Calle Mayor de Triana 39
☎ 928 38 27 32

Food and Drink

Cumbres Canarias
This shop stocks sausages and cheeses produced from all parts of the island.
✉ Avda de las Escaleritas 43
☎ 928 20 45 26 ✉ C/Francisco Gourie ☎ 928 36 78 68

Dulcería Sotomayor
One of the city's top pastry shops.
✉ C/León y Castillo 129

La Garriga
For all delicatessen products.
✉ C/Alvarado 16 ☎ 928 37 17 10

Morales

A traditional café selling delicious cakes and pastries.

✉ C/Viera y Clavijo 4; also at Reyes Catolicos 12 ☎ 928 36 30 18

Handicrafts

Atarecos

The stock here includes Latin American as well as Canarian handicraft and clothes. You can buy a Canarian shepherd's cloak or vaulting pole (*garotte*) or a traditional black felt hat (*cachorro canario*).

✉ C/Peregrina 4 ☎ 928 37 26 28

Ezquerra

The place to buy traditional straw hats, black felt hats and shoes.

✉ C/Travieso 4 ☎ 928 37 07 16

FEDAC

The Fundación para la Etnografía y el Desarollo de la Artesania Canaria is a non-profit public trust for the development of Canarian handicraft and has three outlets on the island. This branch sells decoratively carved bone-handled knives (*naifes*), pottery, traditional musical instruments and basketwork. A woman spins wool by the door to create a suitably artisan ambience.

✉ C/Domingo J Navarro 7 ☎ 928 38 23 60

Leiva

Canarian threadwork and embroidery. The best quality work is of heirloom standard and therefore very expensive.

✉ C/Cano 11 ☎ 928 36 55 42

Orbis

Sr Miguel Santana Cruz specialises in *timples*, a type of small Canarian guitar. Buy off the peg, or get one custom-made.

✉ C/Mayor de Triana 51 ☎ 928 36 81 48

Markets

Mercado de Vegueta

The oldest general market in the city, where you can find abundant fish, meat, fruit and vegetables – the variety of potatoes is astonishing. The market is surrounded by small lively bars and *churrerias* – stalls selling *churros* fritters (a traditional Spanish breakfast).

✉ C/Mendizábal

Mercado del Puerto

Recently renovated market, popular with sailors from ships docked in port. Like most Canarian markets, it stays open from 7am until 2pm.

✉ C/Albareda

Perfumes

Defa

Offers a good selection of cosmetics and perfumes. All the major brands are represented.

✉ Calle Mayor de Triana ☎ 928 36 53 15

Yves Rocher

A huge range of perfumes and beauty goods at very reasonable prices.

✉ C Nestor de la Torre 36 ☎ 928 24 73 89

Tobacco

El Rincón del Fumador

Stocks a range of Canarian cigars and cigarettes.

✉ C/Albareda 48

Marquez

Cigars and cigarettes of all lengths and thicknesses, including those from the island of La Palma, said to be the best among the Canaries.

✉ C/Ripoche 1 ☎ 928 26 56 35

Miguel Santana

A speciality cigar shop.

✉ C/Carmen Quintana 20 ☎ 928 25 61 04

Added Value?

It is no longer true that the Canary Islands are a duty-free haven for bargain-hunters. Admittedly there is no value added tax and there are some minor concessions based on Spain's terms of entry into the European Union. However, these factors do not automatically guarantee low prices.

The South

Resort Shopping

Shopping can be a bizarre experience in the southern resorts because, with the exception of Puerto de Mogán, the activity is concentrated in the giant shopping/restaurant/entertainment malls called *centros comerciales*, rather than in shops on streets. These shopping centres are often huge concrete blocks three to four storeys high, connected by stairs and passages. The shops themselves, with one or two exceptions, appear rather tatty and generally stock a limited range of cheap goods.

Centros Comerciales

Maspalomas
Faro 2

Regarded as the most up-market in the whole San Agustín/Playa del Inglés/Maspalomas complex. One of three centres in Maspalomas, the others being Oasis and Veradero.

✉ Campo Internacional s/n
☎ 928 76 91 97

Playa del Inglés
Yumbo Centrum

This is the biggest commercial centre in the resort. Other centres are Aguila Roja; Alohe; Anexo 11; Cita; El Veril; Gran Chaparral; Kasbah; La Sandia; Metro, Plaza de Maspalomas and Tropical.

✉ Avda Estados Unidos de Norteamérica s/n ☎ 928 76 41 96

San Agustín
San Agustín

A large commercial centre on three floors. There is a smaller one called El Pulpo.

✉ C/ de las Dalias ☎ 928 76 23 71

San Fernando
San Fernando

Along with Botánico, the Mercado Municipal, Nilo and Eurocenter, this is an economical place to shop.

✉ Avda de Tejeda

Handicrafts

Agüimes
Eduardo Ramirez

Unglazed pottery made entirely by hand, without the wheel, in the ancient pre-Spanish tradition of this island, as well as modern pieces and ceramic sculpture.

✉ C/Bolivia 22 ☎ 928 78 49 23

Playa del Inglés
Artesanía Caneria

Following the theory that the same goods are cheaper in San Fernando than they are in Playa del Inglés, handicraft shoppers cross the highway to this craft shop in Local 51.

✉ Centro Comercial San Fernando

La Galería

A shop in the great warren of the Yumbo Centro carrying a range of island handicraft, as well as from further afield. There are occasional gems to be discovered here.

✉ Yumbo Centro

FEDAC

Canarian handicrafts sold at the Tourist Information Office.

✉ Centro Insular de Turismo, Avda de España (on corner with Avda de los Estados Unidos)
☎ 928 76 25 91

Puerto de Mogán
Art Gallery

Self-taught Danish artist and long-term resident of the island Lykke Vigen has three galleries displaying his work in Puerto de Mogán, each of them, it seems, managed by a multi-lingual member of his extended family. The watercolours are charming and unashamedly romantic. A small landscape or flower painting makes an easy-to-carry gift.

✉ Psje de los Pescadores 4a
☎ 928 56 51 36

La Bodeguilla Juananá

A craft shop-cum-restaurant

selling the best – that is, the most authentic Canarian produce, be it ceramic bowls or local cheeses, well displayed. Open 12–4 and 7–midnight, unless the owner has gone fishing, when he leaves a notice on the window to that effect. During summer months, open evenings only. Closed Mon. The restaurant serves nouvelle Canarian cuisine, a far cry from the usual hearty stews.

⊠ **Puerto de Mogán, local 390**
☎ **928 56 50 44**

Rincon Canario
This stylishly decorated shop stocks a wide range of Canarian handicrafts – ceramics, embroidery, basketwork.

⊠ **Puerto de Mogán, local 105**
☎ **928 56 50 26**

Markets

Arguineguín
Fish market
Held every morning. There is also a general market on Tuesday.

⊠ **Arguineguín harbour**

Puerto de Mogán
Fish market
Another daily fish market. Friday is the general market day.

⊠ **Puerto de Mogán harbour**

San Fernando
Wednesday and Saturday markets
A wide range of local goods on sale.

⊠ **Avda Alejandro del Castillo s/n**

Vecindario
Wednesday market
A variety of products sold on the weekly stalls.

⊠ **Avda de Canarias**

Needlework and Embroidery

Ingenio
Aurora Cruz
An interesting selection of embroidered goods and open threadwork in cotton and linen.

⊠ **C/Dr Espino Sanchez**
☎ **928 78 10 77**

Candelaria Artiles
Attractive gifts in traditional style – tablecloths, bed linen, blouses.

⊠ **C/Francisco Perez Ramírez**
☎ **928 78 48 91**

Cooperativa Odalac Oinegni
A wide range of products sold by this cooperative, whose name is Calado Ingenio spelled backwards.

⊠ **C/ Nueva 7** ☎ **928 78 30 37**

Museo de Piedras y Artesania Canaria
Needlework and embroidery from Gran Canaria and the rest of the archipelago as well as basketwork, pottery, herbs and cigars.

⊠ **Camino Real de Gando 1**
☎ **928 78 11 24**

Pottery

Ingenio
Taller Almagre
Look here for Canarian pottery – hand-turned and unglazed.

⊠ **Princesa Guayarmina 2**
☎ **928 78 30 14**

Taller Basalto
Bowls, cups and plates in traditional designs.

⊠ **C/ Felicita Rodrigues 23**
☎ **928 78 49 23**

Bargain Buys
Nobody will be surprised if you bargain over the prices quoted for goods on sale in the *centros comerciales*. You can take the opportunity to haggle over items such as perfumes, leather goods – bags and coats, T-shirts, towels, tablecloths, baseball caps and clothes and electronic products, sold in establishments often owned by Asian traders, known locally as *Hindoos*.

Central & North Gran Canaria

Canarian Music

The *timple* is a small four- or five-stringed Canarian guitar and the *chacara* is the Canarian castanet – both are handcrafted on the island. Since the revival of folk music on the island in the 1970s, traditional music and dance have acquired a special importance. You will find the music of Gran Canaria's most popular folk group, Los Gofiones, in any music shop. For those who want to learn to sing, dance or play in traditional style, the Académia de Folklore Canario La Solana (✉ Paseo de San Antonio, Las Palmas, ☎ 928 25 31 76) will help.

Food and Drink

Arucas
Destilerías Arehucas
Come here for rum, famous produce of Arucas.
✉ Lugar Era de San Pedro 2
☎ 928 60 00 50

Moya
Dorados
Mouthwatering biscuits and cakes, including the traditional *mimos* and *suspiros*.
✉ C/General Franco 19

San Bartolomé de Tirajana
Bar Martin
Guindilla, liqueur made from sour cherries, is on sale at this bar.
✉ C/Reyes Catolicos

Santa María de Guía
Los Quesos
A cheese emporium, assorted produce of sheep and goat's milk plus honey, local wine, rum and a good variety of craftwork.
✉ Carretera General Lomo de Guillén 17, Santa María de Guía
☎ No phone

Santiago Giol
Buy *queso de flor de Guía*, a creamy cheese flavoured with artichoke flowers.
✉ C/Marqués de Muni 34
☎ 928 88 18 75

Tejeda
Dulcería Nublo
Delicious almond sweets and cakes.
✉ C/Dr Hernández Guerra
☎ 928 66 60 30

Telde
El Isleño
A good choice of rum, including the Arehucas and Artemi brands and many island liqueurs.
✉ C General Bravo 39
☎ 928 71 19 00

Vega de San Mateo
Molino San Mateo
Gofio (toasted meal, a traditional part of the Canarian diet) is milled and sold here.
✉ Queipo de Llano 8
☎ 928 66 20 57

Handicrafts

Arucas
Feluco
Small sculptures and objects made of the striking grey basalt stone, *piedra azul*, dug from the local quarries. Picture frames, flowers, a model of the church of San Juan Bautista in Arucas – are all sold here.
✉ C/Dr Fleming ☎ 928 60 54 45

Norberto Marrero
This shop specialises in traditional Canarian knives with decorated handles. Some are intricately patterned with inlaid bone, horn, brass, glass, ceramics, even silver and gold. The rarer the material and the more complicated the decoration, the more expensive.
✉ C/Clavel 8 ☎ 928 88 05 55

Roberto Ramirez
For walking sticks that are not just functional but carved, sculpted, inlaid, bound and generally decorated until they become collectors' pieces; and for extravagantly fanciful kites – this is the place.
✉ C/ Garcia Guerra 2
☎ 928 60 51 73

Gáldar
Juan Aguíar
Come here to buy the *timple*

– a small guitar, a vital instrument in the performance of traditional music.

✉ **Princesa Guayarmina 25**
☎ **928 55 05 35**

Luis Marrero

Cuchillos Canarios (Canarian knives), an essential tool for every Canarian farmer, are sold here as collectors' pieces, due to their decorated handles.

✉ **C/Clavel 8** ☎ **928 88 05 55**

Luis Suárez

Basketwork, made from cane and palm leaves.

✉ **Los Caideros** ☎ **928 55 05 27**

Santa Lucía de Tirajana

Juan Ramírez

A master potter, producing a range of distinctive items.

✉ **C/Leopoldo Matos 37**
☎ **928 64 13 89**

Rosendo Lopez

A good selection of traditional pottery.

✉ **Fernando Guanarteme 45**
☎ **928 75 12 98**

Santa María de Guía

Rafael Torres

An excellent place if you are looking for the traditional, elaborately decorated Canarian knives.

✉ **C/18 de Julio 48**
☎ **928 88 16 09**

Taller de Artesania Guiarte

Juan Jose Caballero works in wood – traditional country tools and objects – bowls, spoons, boxes and stools. He also stocks antiques – and virtually anything else, in fact, as long as it is fashioned out of wood.

✉ **C/Lepanto 9** ☎ **928 88 27 79**

FEDAC

Handicraft shop selling the whole range of embroidery, needlework, pottery and basketwork, sponsored by the island government.

✉ **Parador Cruz de Tejeda**
☎ **928 38 23 60**

Telde

Juan Herrera

Another outlet selling the *timple*, sold ready-made in a range of prices, or custom-made – a very expensive option.

✉ **Carrión, Telde** ☎ **928 69 25 95**

Vega de San Mateo

Carmelo Texeira

A wide range of basketwork items.

✉ **C/Los Chorros 67**
☎ **928 66 18 52**

Markets

Arucas

Saturday market

A busy weekly market, held, as in all major towns, in addition to the permanent municipal market.

✉ **Plaza de la Constitución**

Teror

Sunday market

A fascinating selection of local produce, including marzipan cakes from the nearby convent, and the town's very own sausage, *chorizo rojo*.

✉ **Plaza del Pino**

Vega de San Mateo

Sunday market

Situated in the centre of a richly agricultural community, this market attracts customers from all over the island.

✉ **Avda del Mercado**

Ceramics

Most of the ceramics sold on the island are made in the traditional manner and to traditional designs. These are generally simple objects of everyday use like bowls, plates or jugs. Occasionally you will find copies of pre-Hispanic artefacts, such as the terracotta Mother Earth-type idol figure (the *Ídolo de Tara*), clay pipes (*cachimbas*), or seals in geometric patterns (*pintaderas*), now fashioned into brooches or pins.

Las Palmas & the South

Central Gran Canaria and the North

Any trip to a cave church or a restaurant in a cave (Artenara) is at least a novelty for young people, but there is not much to entertain children in the north or centre, with the exception of Reptilandia Park in Gáldar (✉ Carretera Norte ☎ 928 55 12 69), where poisonous snakes, alligators, lizards and turtles can be seen in a pleasant hillside park, plus a parrot on a perch that calls out 'Hola. Que tal?' ('Hallo. How are you?'), as you approach.

Las Palmas
Casa de Colón

Children who are intrigued by adventure, exploration and ships will love this house where Christopher Columbus once stayed (▶ 18 and 31).

✉ Calle de Colón 1 ☎ 928 31 23 73 🕔 Mon–Fri 9–6, Sat–Sun 9–3. Closed public hols 🚌 30 from Maspalomas, 1 from Parque Santa Catalina

Museo Canario

A museum full of mummies, skulls and skeletons is bound to be a hit with many children (▶ 33).

✉ Calle Dr Chil 25 ☎ 928 31 56 00 🕔 Mon–Fri 10–8, Sat–Sun 10–2. Closed public hols 🚌 30 from Maspalomas, 1 from Parque Santa Catalina

Parque Doramas

Another green space where you can let the children off the leash. They can watch Canarian folk dancing in the Pueblo Canario and remember the sad fate of the early Guanches evoked in the statue outside the Hotel Santa Catalina.

✉ Ciudad Jardín 🚌 30

Parque de San Telmo

There is a children's recreation area in this park, and children might enjoy the tiles and curves of the popular kiosk café (▶ 38).

✉ Corner of Calle Bravo Murillo and Avda Rafael Cabrera 🚌 1, 11, 13, 9

Parque de Santa Catalina

If you are visiting the city during any of the fiestas, particularly if you are here at Carnival, take the children to the special children's shows here, early each evening.

There is music, dancing, laser shows and entertainments on a huge stage (▶ 38).

✉ Santa Catalina ☎ Tourist Information Office 928 26 23 55 🚌 39

Playa de las Canteras

A child-friendly beach is an incomparable advantage in a city where few entertainments are especially provided for children (▶ 23 and 39).

✉ Las Palmas ☎ Tourist Information Office at Parque de Santa Catalina 928 26 46 23 🚌 1, 17, 23

Maspalomas
Aqua Sur

Day-long fun in pools and water slides, at this very popular water park.

✉ Carretera Palmitos Parque km 3 ☎ 928 14 19 05 🕔 Daily, summer 10–6, winter 10–5 🚌 30 from Las Palmas

Camello Safari Dunas

A camel ride is always popular, and an even bigger treat when the progress is through sand dunes. Don't forget the sun hats. Camel safaris are also available in the Fataga and Chamoriscan barrancos.

✉ Avda Dunas s/n ☎ 928 77 20 58 🕔 Daily 9–5 🚌 Plaza del Faro, 29, 30, 32

Gran Karting Maspalomas

For the teenagers, this Go-Kart track near Aqua Sur is a guaranteed success.

✉ Carretera Monte León, km 2 ☎ 928 14 12 38 🚌 45, 70

Holiday World

A funfair with rides for all the family, open in the evening. The entrance ticket entitles you to free rides everywhere except the Laserdrome Battleground. There are plenty of stands for snacks and drinks and enough diversions to keep the entire family entertained.

✉ **Campo Internacional de Maspalomas** ☎ **928 76 07 99**
⏰ **Daily from 5PM summer, 6PM winter** 🚌 **Salcai 29, 30, 32, 36, 45, 70**

Ocean Park

Water slides, wave pool, indoor games. Children can happily spend the whole day here under supervision.

✉ **Campo Internacional de Maspalomas** ☎ **928 76 43 61**
⏰ **Daily from 10AM**

Palmitos Parque

Although children love the performing parrots, this is much more than a parrot park. There is a great new aquarium and attractive snack bars and cafés which serve the sort of food – hamburgers, pizzas – that children prefer.

✉ **Barranco de Chamoriscán**
☎ **928 14 02 76** ⏰ **Daily 9–6**
🚌 **Free bus from Maspalomas**

Playa del Inglés
Mini-Tren

This miniature train chunters through a circular route at Playa del Inglés starting from the El Veril Comercial Centre on Avda Italia. It gives small, tired legs – and big, tired ones, too – a well-earned rest while revealing a different view of the world. The train usually leaves every 30 minutes for a 30-minute trip from Avenida Italia and back again, but the service is run privately and depends on the operator's mood and availability.

Puerto de Mogán
Yellow Submarine

Journey to the bottom of the sea – well, almost. A submarine trip to see a wreck and brilliant marine life.

✉ **Pantalán Dique Sur**
☎ **928 56 51 08** ⏰ **10, 10:50, 11:40, 12:30, 1:30, 2:10, 4, 4:50**
🚌 **Free bus from resorts**

Puerto Rico
Escuela de Vela Joaquín Blanco Torrent

A 13-day summer sailing course for 8- to 15-year-olds with theory and practice classes, plus time off for volleyball, soccer etc. Book via Federación de la Vela.

✉ **Muelle Deportivo, Las Palmas** ☎ **928 29 15 67**

Nautic Safari

A convoy of hi-tech dinghies leaves from Puerto Rico by way of Mogán to Güigüi beach in the west. Once there, jet skis, snorkels and picnics are unloaded and the fun, which includes beach games, begins. A six-hour trip for young people.

✉ **Puerto Escala**
☎ **928 56 09 68**

San Agustín
Gran Karting Club

Not just for adults or big kids, this Go-Kart track – the largest in Spain – even caters for children under five.

✉ **Carretera General del Sur km 46** ☎ **928 15 71 90** ⏰ **Daily, summer 11–10, winter 10–9**

Sioux City

Wild West show with enough jail break-outs, gun-chases, bows and arrows and bullets (fake) for any young person to feel lucky.

✉ **Cañón del Águila** ☎ **928 76 25 73** ⏰ **Daily** 🚌 **Salcai bus 29**

Bull-friendly Fights

A special tourist-geared bullfight takes place every Thursday in Playa del Inglés, when the bull is not harmed (bullfighting is not as popular on the Canary Islands as it is on the mainland).

Las Palmas

Nightlife in Las Palmas
There is something in this city for every taste, however mainstream or bizarre. The general rule is: the nearer you are to the Parque Santa Catalina and the later at night, the nearer you are to topless bars, sex shows and to nightlife of a generally *louche* nature. That is not to suggest, however, that there are no wild night-time entertainments in the Old Town or that you will not find a quiet place to sip a mineral water in a Santa Catalina bar. The venues for young nightlife change with every season. The signs are that the trendiest clubs are in the Las Arenas *centro comercial* and around the marina at Las Palmas. If you turn up at a bar or disco before 10PM, you will find yourself alone.

Films

Every other year, in October and November, the Arts Council of the Island Government sponsors an International Film Festival. Most cinemas show mainstream international feature films – mostly from the US and dubbed into Spanish.

Cine Capitol
A regular changing programme of mainstream films.
✉ **Paseo Tomás Morales 25**
☎ **928 36 61 68**

Multicines Galaxy's
A popular multi-screen cinema.
✉ **C/ El Cid 53** ☎ **928 22 44 74**

Multicines La Ballena
Based in the shopping and entertainment complex by the southern exit out of town. Mostly foreign and dubbed mainstream films.
✉ **La Ballena Centro Comercial** ☎ **928 42 03 35**

Multicines Royal
Another cinema offering a choice of screens and mainstream films.
✉ **C/León y Castillo 40**
☎ **928 36 09 54**

Folk Dancing

Pueblo Canario
Many cultures have contributed to the folk dancing styles of Gran Canaria, not least the Spanish, Portuguese and Latin American. The *isa* is a lively, energetic dance, the *folía*, slower and more languorous, *el canario*, a group dance, and all are accompanied by music played on traditional instruments, twice weekly in the Canarian Village. The folk costumes, now worn on rare formal occasions, differ from village to village, but they are all splendidly colourful.
✉ **Parque Doramas**
🕐 **Performances Sun 11:45, 1:15; Thu 5:30, 7** 🚌 **30**

Nightclubs and Bars

Casino de las Palmas
The smartest place on the island to risk your fortune, or watch someone else risk theirs on black jack, *chemin de fer*, baccarat, roulette, etc. Formal dress is obligatory. Take your passport.
✉ **Santa Catalina Hotel, Parque Doramas** ☎ **928 24 30 40**

Chistera
A pub with live music and stand-up comics, for visitors whose Spanish is up to it. The patron is comedian, Manolo Vieira.
✉ **C/Manuel Durán 3**
☎ **928 22 47 77**

Cuasquías
Smart and lively venue for all age groups to see and hear top performers. Good jazz and Latin American music.
✉ **C/San Pedro 2, near Triana**
☎ **928 37 00 46** 🕐 **From 10:30PM**

Destilería
A lively, popular place with the young of Las Palmas for drinks and a dance.
✉ **C/Perdomo 20** 🕐 **From 10:30PM**

El Coto
As you would expect of a discotheque in the Hotel Melia, the ambience is

elegant and the atmosphere refined – even on a Saturday night. The music is international/Latin American.

✉ C/Gomera 6 ☎ 928 22 63 59

El Patio Peregrina

A bar and quiet music on a lovely interior patio.

✉ C/Peregrina 1 ☎ 928 36 40 63

El Tren

A long, narrow bar with live music and a welcome for all ages.

✉ C/Domingo de Navarro 19
🕐 Mon–Thu from 9PM, Fri–Sat from 10PM. Closed Sun

Equ

A lively bar, walls covered in videos; attracts a young crowd.

✉ C/ Nicolás Estévanez 24 (corner of C/Secretario Artiles)
☎ 928 22 20 46

Floridita

A large new restaurant/bar in the Triana district has become very popular very quickly. Locals love the Cuban ambience and rhythm.

✉ C/Remedios 10–12 ☎ 928 43 17 40

Neon

Dancing to an old-fashioned orchestra. Near Playa de las Canteras.

✉ C/Luis Morote 61 ☎ 928 22 34 71 🕐 Daily 9–3

Pacha

Smart disco with a giant video screen. Live music on the terrace.

✉ C/Simón Bolivár 3
☎ 928 22 91 47

Piano Bar Sargent Pippers

Live music, popular with older crowd near Playa de las Canteras.

✉ C/Alfredo Jones 41
☎ 928 27 16 84

Toca Toca

Trendy folk congregate here at dawn to dance. Music is loud and up-to-date.

✉ Secretario Artiles 53
☎ 928 36 12 23

Utopia

A rather stark environment which comes into its own only after 3AM.

✉ C/ Tomás Miller 42
☎ 928 27 77 79

Theatre and Concerts

Auditorio Alfredo Krans

A major new venue for classical music concerts and a conference centre right on the beach with great sea views.

✉ Paseo de las Canteras s/n
☎ 928 49 17 70

Centro Insular de Cultura (Arts Centre)

Gran Canaria's venue for concerts, exhibitions and lectures. Many of the events are shared with Santa Cruz de Tenerife, and there is information about festivals and cultural activities taking place on the other Canary Islands available here.

✉ Primero de Mayo
☎ 928 37 10 11

Teatro Pérez Galdós

Home to the island's symphony orchestra and operatic society, the theatre also hosts visits from groups, orchestras and performers of international standing, such as the Boston Symphony and the Los Angeles Philharmonic orchestras.

✉ C/Lentini 1 ☎ 928 36 15 09
🚌 1, 9, 11, 12

Music, Ballet, Opera and Theatre

An International Music Festival is held every year in Las Palmas, in January and early February. March and April see the Festival of Opera, and in April and May, the International Festival of Ballet and Dance is celebrated, including performances of Spanish light opera called *zarzuelas*.

The South, Centre & North

Disco Life

Discos, pubs and nightlife in general are concentrated in the *centros comerciales* – the commercial centres, of which there are many in the southern resorts. German and British entertainers often perform in bars and pubs to their own national clientele. Centro Comercial Kasbah, Playa del Inglés, is the most popular for dancing or listening to music: try Malibu, Fantasy, Rainbow or Garaje. Centro Comercial Metro, Playa del Inglés, has a solid following among young people at Pachá, Joy, Terraza El Metro. Centro Comercial Yumbo, Playa del Inglés, attracts a gay crowd to bars and discos like Gay Male, King's Club and Come Back.

Island Wisdom

Ana Stromberg Heirera, a Swedish resident, can advise visitors on walking routes, obtaining fishing licences and virtually any other local information, and can be reached at Martina 928 22 (56 20 67).

Nightlife
San Agustín
Casino Tamarindos Palace
You have to be over 18, look respectable (that is, wear jacket and tie if you are male) and carry identification to gamble or watch. There is also a cabaret show of dancing girls – and some dancing men, too – in feathers and sequins.

✉ **Hotel Tamarindos, C/Las Retamas, San Agustín**
☎ **928 76 68 28**

Sport
Diving
Puerto Rico
Aquanauts Dive Center
Run by a Finnish company which offers daily dives, night dives on Sun and Thu and full-day dives (two tanks) plus introductory courses for learners.

☎ **928 56 06 55**

Top Diving
Maximum capacity, 16 people. Leaving at 9AM and 2PM to a variety of dive destinations, including caves, reefs and wrecks.

☎ **928 71 48 38**

Fishing
Puerto de Mogán
Billfish Fever 11
Although the company is based in Puerto de Mogán, the boat leaves for high seas and deep-water fishing trips from Puerto Rico.

☎ **928 56 50 95** ⚓ **Boats leave 9AM return 3PM**

Puerto Rico
Alcor 111
The skipper offers sport and deep-water fishing for tuna, shark, white and blue swordfish. Bring your own lunch. Alcor 1V and Spica 11 also available.

☎ **928 73 59 06** ⚓ **Boats depart 9AM, return at 3PM**

Barakuda 11
Sport and high seas fishing trip, sandwiches and drinks provided plus tackle and bait. The skipper can provide instruction in Spanish, English, French and German. Book two days ahead.

☎ **928 73 50 80** ⚓ **Daily 9AM–1PM**

Flying
San Agustín
Real Aero Club de Gran Canaria
Light aircraft to hire. The Club also runs a pilot's school. If you are starting from scratch, it will take you 3–4 months to get a pilot's licence. Free-fall and ordinary parachuting also offered.

✉ **Carretera General del Sur km 46.5** ☎ **928 15 71 47**
⚓ **Daily by appointment**

Golf
Caldera de Bandama
Club de Golf Bandama
Splendid location on the edge of the Bandama crater, near Santa Brígida: 18 holes, par 71, 5,679m course. Hotel and restaurant attached. Visitors, as temporary members, may play, except on Sundays. Riding school attached.

✉ **Carretera de Bandama s/n**
☎ **928 35 10 50** 🚌 **39**

Maspalomas
Campo de Golf
Close to dunes and palm groves, this is another splendidly sited golf course: 18 holes, par 73, 6,220m course. Visitors may book lessons, hire clubs and practise on the

driving range. Two more golf courses are currently planned for the island.

✉ Avda Neckerman s/n ☎ 928 76 25 81 📋 30

Mountain Biking
Playa del Inglés
Happy Biking

Bikes can be hired from one to six days. There are special weekend rates. Tours of varying difficulty are also on offer and prices include hire of bike, helmet, gloves, picnic and insurance. Rollerblades can be hired by the hour or day.

✉ Yumbo Centrum, ground floor ☎ 928 76 82 98

Riding
Bandama
Bandama Golf Club Riding School

Associated with the golf club, this horse-riding school offers lessons and organised treks in a dramatic rural landscape.

✉ Carretera de Bandama s/n ☎ 928 35 12 90

Palmitos Parque
Rancho Park

Lessons and rides in the Barranco de Chamoriscán, 8–1 daily except Mon and Thu (5–8).

✉ Carretera de Palmitos Parque s/n ☎ 928 76 68 74

Sailing
Maspalomas
Club Nautico de Maspalomas

Sailing lessons and boat hire.

✉ Pasito Blanco ☎ 928 76 76 83

Puerto de Mogán
Paradise Yachting

A range of water sports, including sailing, offered

here: choice of monohull or catamaran, with or without a skipper.

✉ Local 96 ☎ 928 56 55 90

Walking
Maspalomas
Municipal Walks

The San Bartolomé de Tirajana municipal tourist office publishes leaflets of 'Touristic Footpaths' – proposed walks, illustrated with maps and with full directions.

✉ Plaza de las Constitucíon 1 ☎ 928 14 06 64

Playa del Inglés
Gran Canarias Natural

This company offers a whole day's walk ending with a barbecue. There is a choice of 10 walking routes, lasting from four to seven-and-a-half hours, of varying difficulty. Book through your hotel reception, or telephone.

☎ 928 75 39 49

Windsurfing

Most beaches have equipment to hire and offer lessons to beginners and those wishing to improve.

Playa del Águila
F2 Surfcenter Dunkerbeck

Eugen Dunkerbeck runs a windsurf school for beginners and provides facilities for those with advanced skills.

✉ Plaza de Hibiscus, Águila Playa ☎ 928 76 29 58

Playa De Tarajalillo
Club Mistral Canarias

Rents boards all year round and offers lessons to beginners during the summer.

✉ In the hotel Bahía Feliz ☎ 928 77 40 25

Name-calling

Canarios consider themselves to be different from mainland Spaniards, whom they call 'Peninsulares'. Occasionally, when they feel less than kind, they refer to them as 'Godos' or Goths. You may see signs saying: 'Afuera Godos' – 'Goths Go Home'.

Island Walkers

Walking in the mountains is a popular activity on Gran Canaria, particularly with the younger generation. Older folk remember a time when there were few roads on the island and walking was the only method of transport. Not surprisingly, they prefer to ride in motorcars. Caminos Reales, literally 'royal ways', are a network of paths once guaranteed by royal authority. They now form the basis of much of the island's walking tracks.

What's On When

Festivals
Gran Canaria has a wealth of festivals. Before Carnival is the Almond Blossom Festival; after Carnival is Holy Week. Then there are the anniversaries of the Spanish conquest, the ancient aboriginal festivities and the great island pilgrimage to Teror. That's not counting all the festivals associated with the produce of the earth – of *gofio*, apricots – and the sea, and the celebrations of the saints' days of each town and village.

January
Festival of the Three Kings, 6 January: gifts for the children

February
Almond Blossom Festival, Tejeda and Valsequillo: song and dance, picnics, almond sweets and cakes
Carnival: street bands, parties and parades

March
Arguineguín celebrates the feast day of Santa Agueda

April
Fiesta de los Aborigenes commemorates the defeat of the aboriginal people at Fortaleza de Ansite on 29 April. Celebrations marking the conquest of the islands are held in Las Palmas

May
Apricot Festival in Fataga

June
Feast of Corpus Cristi (sometimes in May): the streets are decorated with flowers and sand
Anniversary of the foundation of Las Palmas

July
Fiestas del Carmen are celebrated by all fishing villages, 16 July
Feast day of Santiago, 25 July, Gáldar and San Bartolomé. Gáldar has Canarian wrestling, *romerias* (picnics) and traditional dancing

August
Bajada de la Rama celebrated in Agaete, 4 August, is probably the most popular festival on the island. From an ancient aboriginal rite of praying for rain. Local people climbed high into the pine forests and brought down branches to thrash the sea. Modern Canarios do the same. A great opportunity to get wet and have a party

September
Feast of La Virgen del Pino (Our Lady of the Pine) in Teror, the patron saint of the whole island, 8 September. Pilgrims come from all over the island, many of them walking through the night to Teror. They may bring cartfuls of produce, which are placed before the image of the Virgin in the square and then dispensed to poor folk later
Fiesta del Charco in San Nicolás de Tolentino, 10 September. Everybody gets wet – probably another relic of an early aboriginal rite

October
Fiestas de Nuestra Señora del Rosario (Our Lady of the Rosary), celebrated in Agüimes, 5 October, with Canarian stick-fighting and wrestling
La Naval, 6 October in Las Palmas, commemorates the successful repulsion of the English privateer, Francis Drake, from the islands in 1595

November
Festival of San Martín de Porres, Arinaga

December
Fiesta de los Labradores, Santa Lucía, 20 December: people celebrate by dressing in peasant costume and carrying old-fashioned farming tools
Feast Day of Santa Lucia, 13 December, a joint Swedish and Canarian celebration in Santa Lucia